D1602234

POTWORKS:
A FIRST BOOK OF CLAY

Potworks
A First Book of Clay
by Billie Luisi

William Morrow & Company, Inc.
New York 1973

Luisi, Billie.
    Potworks: a first book of clay.

    Bibliography: p.
    1. Pottery.   I. Title.
TP808.L74   738.1   72-12711
ISBN 0-688-00144-0
ISBN 0-688-05144-8 (pbk)

For A. Douglas Simpson

1734407

ACKNOWLEDGMENTS

I'd like to thank Lou Talento, Pat Dougan, Janet and Bernie Toy, and Bob and Harriet Barrett, for their help and patience in backing me up during the actual writing of this book. They've all helped and made suggestions and most generously put up with me and the manuscript through all the changes.

And I'd like to thank all the good souls who helped get it going on Fifth Street that first year: Joanna and Lenny, Carmen, Bob Bailin, Bob April, and Murray Hochman, and all the people in the caverns at 225 East Fifth who helped keep it afloat through the last year there: Lou, Pat, Terry, Bob, Jenny, Tucker, and Frances, whose screaming did keep the junkies at bay. Peace wherever you are.

Billie Luisi

Bearsville, N.Y., winter of 1971.

THE BODY OF THE BOOK

INTRODUCTORY

This book is for lovers of fire and earth everywhere. It has been made with a great deal of help from my friends. I've tried to write a book to help all the hidden potters out there, outside the system, who labor with no teachers, masters, potteries, suppliers, or knowledgeable friends. I'm trying to make some experiential information available in a cheap, accessible form. I've tried to simplify the technical stuff so that it is comprehensible and useful, and to make people conscious of the great amount of clay tradition and experience out beyond the isolated, beginning potter. All that can be absorbed then as you grow. Most of the help in this book deals with ways to get on with it, the *it* being the hidden drudgework involved with clay, the part no one told you about that first day you sat down to your first wheel and lump of sticky stuff. I've tried to stay away from telling you how-to and what kind of things to make in clay. That's up to you.

What is in this book and what is not. There are several parts to this whole. The first is an overly long wordlist, intended to deal with the problem of jargon. Most good books on ceramics have one, but it is in the back. Mine is up front. When you get through the wordlist, you will find a list of what you will need. Then you will get to the body of the book. To round it off there are some more lists, improving books, suppliers, things like that.

There are no step-by-step instructions for coil-building, slab-building, or pinch-potting. I go into these briefly, but you can intuit all that or get it from any (that means any: good, bad, indifferent) book on pottery.

There are no step-by-step instructions for throwing. Two good manuals are listed in the booklist (they're illustrated). Throwing is best taught by live demo, films, videotapes, anything graphic. If a live potter is nowhere to be found on your mountain, go to the photo books and be very hard on yourself. Practice at least two hours every day, etc., etc. You need daily access to a wheel if you are going to teach yourself to throw.

There is no encouraging bullshit about ceramics being easy, groovy, organic, by just getting into it. There's plenty of that in other books. And there are no pretty pictures of pots. Publishers dig photoplate albums in craftsy books in order to command big prices. Looking at pots in the round, even in those little glass cages in museums, means much more than pages of plates.

What is in this book is a compilation of experienced details that, I think, will get you on the first step of the journey. Potting is full of mechanical details that have to be learned, assimilated, and accomplished with great energy efficiency, if good pots are to be created. There's seven years' experience of what I call closet potting. Primarily I've written a book for people who wish to pot and find themselves without teachers, facilities, and in pretty awful potting circumstances.

If you love clay and know little about it, there's probably something in this book you need. At the end of the reading, you will know more about working with the stuff you love. I hope it helps you make good things in clay.

WORDLIST

ACID—For ceramic purposes, one of the three major families of glaze ingredients. Silica (SiO_2) is the acid of prime importance to potters. The other glaze component groupings are the neutrals and bases. The acid grouping is often referred to as the RO_2 group (for its radical, RO_2). The main function of the RO_2 group is as glass-formers.

ALKALIS—These are the bases referred to above. Alkaline compounds, such as those of sodium (Na) or potassium (K), are essential in the chemistry of glazing and clay bodies, primarily for their fluxing capabilities.

ALUMINA—Alumina (Al_2O_3) is the primary neutral of interest to the potter. It is tough, very heat-resistant (melting near 3275°F.), and crucial in the formation of glazes and clay bodies.

ASH—Vegetable (wood) ash was commonly used as a glaze at high temperatures. Ashes contribute silica, alumina, and fluxes such as lime and potash to glazes.

BAFFLES—These are deflecting structures inside kilns. They are used to deflect the intense heat coming out of the burners away from the ware and into the chamber in channels that promote good heat circulation.

BASES—See "alkalis" above.

BATS—Plaster, bisqued clay, unfinished wood, or other porous material—circles, slabs, bowls—used for drying wet clay and atop the wheel head in throwing.

BATCH—It is the compounded glaze in its raw state; a group of raw glaze materials that are intended to mature at a specific temperature, and are weighed out proportionately and dispersed evenly.

BISQUE—Once-fired, unglazed ware; for the purposes of this text "bisque" always refers to a low-fired, porous, immature, unglazed ware that doesn't hold water. "Bisque firing" refers here only to the preliminary, first firing to a low temperature, aimed at driving off chemically combined water.

BLISTERING—A glaze fault characterized by cratered surfaces, commonly produced by applying glaze too thickly. Blistering also occurs when lead glazes are subjected to reducing atmospheres.

CASTING—This is a method of shaping liquid clay into objects by the use of molds. It is the major process in the industrialized mass production of pottery. Numerous detailed descriptions of the process are available. Consult works in the booklist. If casting is your major interest or need, turn to that section and skip this book.

CELADON—This term is applicable to an enormously diverse group of high-fired stoneware or porcelain glazes of a feldspathic nature, which employ iron oxide as the basic pigmenting agent and have been fired in a reducing atmosphere. The glazes may be gray, gray-green, pale blue-white, olive, or one of many subtle cool colors. Most of the classic celadons are of Oriental provenance.

CENTERING—In the narrow sense, this is the process of urging your clay mass to the center of the spinning potter's wheel. The recalcitrant clay lump must be forced to hang into the middle of the wheel, over the axle. In this way, you deny centrifugal force its due and can open up the spinning mass and proceed to throw hollow forms.

CHUCK—This is a support used when trimming the bottoms of narrow-necked pots, such as bottles.

CHÜN—Another classic Oriental glaze of an opalescent, thick, cloudy blue or blue-green nature. It is often dramatically splashed with violet or red-purple (reduced copper oxide).

CLAY BODIES—Mixes of clays blended with specific traits, purposes, and maturation temperatures in mind.

COILS—"Snakes" of clay used to build pottery vessels by hand. Coiling is one of the oldest and most basic methods of making clay vessels and was the essential technique in societies where the potter's wheel was unknown.

CONES—Visible devices used to measure and indicate the heat inside a kiln chamber. The pyrometric cones are made up of clays and glaze materials blended to flux and thereby change shape or bend, on a standardized scale, as specific temperatures are reached inside a kiln. Physically, the potter sees the elongated conical shapes bend at target temperatures. In this way, you have a visible, immediate indicator of temperature available to you for guidance. In practice, the potter watches the cones he has set up through the kiln's peepholes. When the "target" or "firing" cone goes down, bends or flattens out, the potter ends his firing cycle.

CRACKING—Opening a kiln very slightly after a firing.

CRAWLING—A glaze fault characterized by separated globules of glaze on the pot's surface and exposed, unglazed-looking areas. It is usually a result of overly thick glaze applications or the presence of dust or other particulate matter on bisque. When bisque ware is dusty, glaze can't adhere properly.

CRAZING—An unintended network of cracks in a glaze, often an indication of tension or lack of fit between clay body and glaze. Its respectable cousin is *crackling*, an *intentional* utilization of the network of cracks (developed through the same kinds of tensions) for specific decorative effect.

CUTTING OFF—Separating your thrown pots from the wheel head or a larger mass of clay. It is done by cutting under the foot of the thrown pot with a length of twisted wire or other tool, and lifting gently on the thrown piece—a very delicate business.

CYLINDERS—What beginning potters make over and over and over again to achieve disciplined control over clay on the revolving wheel.

DAMP BOX, DAMP CLOSET—Unfinished, wet clay pieces must be stored in a situation that doesn't allow any overly rapid drying. Even, slow drying is best for large or widely extended pieces. A corner, closet, or bin, that is closed off and moisture-proof, rustproof, and warp-free, provides the best storage for pieces in process. If the area can be filled with a plaster floor or many plaster bats, the latter can be watered and the whole structure kept evenly humid and damp.

DAMPER—The sliding panel or shutter used to control the draft or oxygen flow in a fuel-burning kiln.

DIPPING—A hand method of applying wet glaze to pots. It consists of immersing pots in the glaze. It is much used by studio potters, as opposed to painting or spraying.

DRAW TRIAL—Before the introduction of standardized pyrometric cones, draw trials were the major visible temperature indicators used by potters. A draw trial is a test ring of clay that is placed in the kiln during stacking in such a position as to enable the potter to reach it with a hook through a peephole or other port. While the firing progresses, the potter hooks out the various rings and toward the end examines them for signs of clay or glaze maturation. They are still much used in salt-glaze firings and other situations where the kiln atmosphere precludes accurate observation of pyrometric cones.

DUNTING—Cracking of pots during the cooling of a kiln, caused by sudden entry of cooler air into the warm kiln.

EARTHENWARE—Pots with a porous clay body, that have been fired to low temperatures.

ELEMENTS—Coiled metal wires of heat-resistant alloys that carry current through electric kilns and generate heat through their resistance capability.

ENAMELS—Low-temperature, colored glaze compounds that are applied over higher-fired, harder, glazed wares.

ENGOBES—Colored clays used for decorative purposes; same as *slips*.

EPSOM SALTS—Magnesium sulfate, used to keep glaze ingredients suspended in water, thus preventing settling of glaze chemicals.

FELDSPARS—Naturally occurring complex compounds that contain alumina, silica, potassium, soda, and other oxides. They come from weathered granitic rock crystals and occur in many diverse, natural combinations. They are a cheap, abundant, nonsoluble source of glaze fluxes. However, since they also contain alumina and silica (which fuse only at very high temperatures), their fluxing capability is limited at low temperatures. They become extremely important fluxes when you get into high-temperature firing. Feldspars are often used as fluxes in clay bodies.

FIRING—The process of heating up the potter's kiln.

FLUE—The exit channel for flame and gases in a fuel-burning kiln; leads to the chimney in a downdraft type of kiln. It may lead into another chamber in a complex type of kiln.

FLUX—A chemical that melts easily and promotes the breakdown and melting of the more heat-resistant contributors in a glaze mix.

FRIT—A pre-fired, pulverized mixture of glaze ingredients, prepared in this way so as to eliminate problematic features of certain useful compounds that are difficult to handle raw; such as toxic oxides (lead), or valuable but soluble alkalis.

GLAZE—A glaze is a glass that has been adjusted to stick onto a clay pot. Chemically, it is usually made up of silica, a flux, and alumina.

GLOBAR—A silicon-carbide rod used as elements in high-firing electric kilns. Globars can go up to cone 18. Kilns utilizing globars must employ transformers.

GRAM SCALE—A device for measuring weight on the metric system.

GREENWARE—Raw ware; unfired pots.

GROG—A pre-fired, high-temperature clay product that is pulverized and made available in a great variety of particle sizes, from very fine to extra coarse. It is mixed into clay bodies to reduce shrinkage, open up the bodies for the outward bound hot gases during firings, to add strength, and at times, simply for texture.

GUMS—Natural, organic substances used to bind glaze mixtures to vessels. Some gums aid in keeping glaze ingredients suspended in water. Gums used for these purposes are gum arabic or gum tragacanth.

HIGH-TEMPERATURE—A matter of debate and personal taste. Potters who are primarily interested in reduction fired stoneware tend to regard cone 8 or 2300°F. and above as "high-temperature." Feldspars tend to act as natural fluxes above this temperature and slip clays fuse to form natural glazes (with no additions) in this range. I tend to feel any temperature above 2000°F. is high. Above cone 4 some low-fire fluxes lose their importance or even become fugitive; glazes tend to look and act more like stoneware glazes of the 2300°F. range, utilize spars extensively, are hard and durable, and begin to chemically meld with the clay body. Since nickel-chrome alloy elements cannot withstand temperatures above 2000°F., I tend to use that as a cutoff line.

INSULATING BRICK—A porous, lightweight, soft but highly refractory (heat-resistant) material that prevents heat transfer. It is commonly used to line kiln walls, doors, lids, etc., and is the dominant material in kiln construction today. It is available in several gradations of insulating capacity, i.e., bricks that withstand 2300°F. as a working temperature, or 2600°F., or 2800°F., etc.

KANTHAL—A metal alloy used for elements in electric kilns that can withstand heats up to 2400°F.

KAOLIN—A primarily white clay that is highly refractory, usually non-plastic, and contains few mineral impurities such as iron oxide. Kaolin approximates the theoretic formula for pure clay ($Al_2O_3 \cdot 2SiO_2 \cdot 2H_2O$), and forms the basis for porcelain clay bodies. It is important in glaze chemistry as a source of alumina. Its importance in ceramic history can't ever be overstated.

KILN—An insulated structure that contains and conserves heat. It's a great deal more complicated than that in practice, but that is the one essential concept to grasp.

KILN WASH—A refractory, creamy paint made up of water and equal parts by weight of kaolin and silica. It is painted on shelves and kiln floors to serve as a protective coating. It protects kiln furnishings from damage because of glaze accidents.

KNEADING—The hand preparation of clay aimed at securing a relatively air-free, homogeneous mass. Spiral kneading: the twisting of clay into densely packed spirals promotes increased plasticity and is the proper preparation of clay intended for use on the wheel.

LEATHERHARD—A stage of raw ware wherein much of the water has dried but the clay is still soft enough to be added onto, manipulated somewhat, carved into, or treated decoratively.

LUSTER—A decorative glazing technique based on metallic salt compounds that are applied to pre-glazed wares and refired to a low temperature, just hot enough to melt the metal on the surface of the pot.

LOW-TEMPERATURE—Again, this is a relative or subjective matter. I regard anything below 2000°F. as a low temperature. A pastry cook would find that mad.

MAT—A pottery glaze surface that is not glossy, but pleasant to the fingertips. Don't confuse mat with underfired. Mats are promoted by the inclusion of $BaCO_3$ or alumina in glazes, in substantial quantities.

MATURE—Hardness, density, and nonporosity add up to maturity in a clay body. A glaze is mature when it is totally fused, hard, and stable.

MATURATION POINT—The temperature at which clay and glazes reach their complete development or maturity, as defined above. Every clay and glaze has its own or appropriate maturation point.

OPENING—Entering the centered, spinning clay mass with your thumb, two fingers, or entire fist, should the mass be large, and pulling out toward the perimeter across the bottom of the clay mass.

OPEN BODY—A clay body that has had grog or other tempering material added to it to create channels for the outward passage of steam and hot gases during the firing. Such a clay body is essential in the building and firing of large sculptural ceramic pieces and in *raku* pottery.

OPEN FIRING—A type of natural-fuel firing wherein the flames have direct access to the ware, and are not blocked by a muffle or other protective structure.

OVERGLAZE—Decorative technique that uses specially prepared colors compounded of coloring oxides, fluxes and a siccative. Usually the overglaze colors are applied to a hard, pre-fired, glazed surface and then refired at a lower temperature. Many colors are based on oxides that are fugitive at high temperatures. Refiring with overglaze colors permits the use of otherwise volatile oxides. See "enamels" above.

OXIDATION—A chemical interaction characterized by the combining of oxygen with another element.

OXIDIZING—A type of fire utilized by potters to heat (or fire) their wares. During an oxidizing fire, oxygen combines with carbon to produce carbon dioxide and heat energy. This reaction is also known as burning or combustion. It releases heat energy, which the potter conserves and accumulates in a kiln, to the point where clay matures. An oxidizing fire is characterized by complete combustion of the available carbon, or fuel. There is, in an oxidizing fire, always enough oxygen available for that complete reaction. The physical characteristics of an oxidizing fire are a clear, smokeless atmosphere and a slight suction in toward the kiln. For a discussion of the electric kiln and oxidation firing take a look at the chapter "Kilns and Firings."

PEEPHOLE—A hole through which you can look and see where your firing is at. It is a small opening in the kiln wall which you plug up during the firing. When you have to check the cones or kiln atmosphere, you pull the plug out and spy in. If you're doing a reduction firing, watch out for flames at the peeps.

PLASTICITY—That incomparable, sacred quality of clay which allows it to be formed and shaped without sag or collapse.

PORCELAIN—A hard, dense, resonant-when-struck, very high-fired clay ware. It varies from white to light gray in body color. Some porcelain is translucent. Usually the clay body and glaze are physically bound and so chemically near one another that you cannot tell where one ends and the other begins.

POURING—Another hand method of glaze application used by studio potters.

POTTERY—A place to pot in. Technically, any low-fired ware.

PUG MILL—A clay-mixing machine that is made up of a trough into which water and dry clay or wet, reconditioned clay, are placed. Blades revolve and churn and compress the clay until it is a homogeneous mix. The clay is then squeezed out a narrow opening at the other end of the machine. The mix can be prepared so as to be almost completely ready for immediate use. I usually age it. I recommend laying it out for some drying (if needed), wedging, kneading. I store it for a couple of weeks to aid plasticity evolution.

PYROMETER—An instrument for measuring heat. I don't recommend dependence upon the pyrometers built into hobbyist's kilns. For accurate temperature indices, use cones.

REDUCING, REDUCTION—A reducing fire is one that is starved for oxygen. This situation arises when the potter cuts back on the air supply or when he increases the carbon input during a firing. The oxygen decrease forces the excess carbon in the kiln atmosphere to hunt for a supply of oxygen. The carbon finds its needed oxygen in the metallic oxides present in the clay and glazes of the wares. It then snatches up whatever oxygen it can get and in this way reduces the metallic oxides to their base metals. The metallic oxides yield their oxygen to the combustion process. Carbon robbing the oxygen makes the glazes and clay bodies look different from wares fired in an oxidizing atmosphere.

REFRACTORY—Having the capability to resist high temperatures. Some important, highly refractory substances potters deal with constantly are: silica, kaolin, alumina, and heat-resistant clays such as fireclay.

SAGGARS—Protective containers made of refractory clays (such as fireclays) that are used as kiln furnishings. Their specific purpose is to protect wares from open flame and combustion gases in natural-fuel fired glaze operations.

SALT GLAZE—A glaze produced by throwing large amounts of common table salt into a hot kiln. The sodium chloride must be introduced when the fire is nearing the clay's maturation point. The salt vaporizes and the sodium combines with free silica of the clay to produce a thin glaze on the ware's surfaces. The glaze has an attractive orange peel-like texture that is peculiar to this process. There is currently a great revival of interest in salting among studio potters.

SHRINKAGE—The contraction of a clay mass caused by both the loss of its physically combined water in drying and the loss of its chemically combined water in firing. In other words, pots get smaller.

SIEVING—The process of putting dry or wet glaze ingredients or clays through a wire mesh screen.

SLAKE—Soaking in an excess of water. It's necessary when you recondition or prepare clay.

SLIP—A clay (or mixture of clays and other raw materials) in suspension; usually used for decorative purposes. In reference to casting technique, the term applies to clay in a liquid (as opposed to a plastic and workable form) state. The clay, suspended in a considerable amount of water, is then poured into molds. When referring to decorative slips, some authors interchange the word "engobe."

SLIP GLAZE—A type of glaze based upon a naturally occurring, single clay that contains enough flux, alumina, and silica to provide a true glaze that needs no further additions. The prominent example of this type of glaze is the famous Albany slip glaze that was employed by nineteenth-century Northeastern stoneware potters.

SPRAYING—A method of glaze application that utilizes a compressed-air spray setup. It is a primary industrial technique of glaze application, producing uniform and unbeatably predictable results.

SPARS—Short for feldspars.

SOAK—To maintain a kiln temperature at one specific level for an extended period of time in order to promote an even heat saturation throughout the chamber, usually at the end of a glaze firing.

STACKING—The loading of a kiln.

STONEWARE—A high-temperature clay ware which is dense, hard, nonporous, and durable. The clays utilized and the firing techniques employed are related to the processes of other high-fired wares such as porcelain. The clays, however, are usually more plastic to work with than are porcelain clay bodies, and from a chemical point of view, contain more metallic impurities, such as iron, than do porcelain bodies.

TEMPERATURE—Heat intensity or the lack of it.

THROW—To make clay shapes through the use of the potter's wheel.

TURNING—Trimming off the excess clay from the foot of a thrown pot. When the pot is leatherhard it is turned upside down, centered, wedged down to the wheel head with wads of clay, and then trimmed.

UNDERFIRING—Not achieving the temperature in your kiln necessary to mature the ware or your glazes.

VITRIFICATION—See "mature" above. The achieving of glassiness or a dense crystalline structure in a clay body or glaze. It makes the ware nonporous.

VOLATIZATION—Changing a solid into a liquid and then into a gas. Certain compounds, such as lead oxides, react this way when subjected to high heats.

WARPAGE—Distortion caused by uneven or rapid drying or uneven firing conditions.

WATERSMOKING—The first part of a firing, up to about 1000°F., during which physically and chemically combined water escapes and carbonaceous matter in the clay or kiln burns out. Since gases are escaping during this period, great care must be taken to increase heat slowly. Sudden heat increases will force these gases into trying to get out rapidly—explosively, if they have to do it that way.

WEDGING—Cutting of clay into pieces and forceful recombining of the pieces, by throwing them at each other to slam out the air in the clay. I find spiral kneading does this more effectively and with less noise pollution. Many potters regard kneading as "wedging." All this activity takes place on a dense, porous-surfaced table, called a wedging table. I like plaster tables best for this.

WHEEL—The potter's basic production machine for making quantities of ware—until the Industrial Revolution.

What You Will Need:

Energy Source: for ceramic purposes; electric
power or a fuel (gas, oil, wood, coal)
Clay
Kiln
Glaze chemicals, and pigmenting oxides
Scales: one triple beam balance gram scale,
one pound scale
Pyrometric cones
Plaster, maybe hundreds of pounds
Plywood
Other wood
Running water, if possible
Sieves
Bowls, buckets, basins
Rags
Old clothes
Plastic garbage cans, or galvanized tin
(20-gallon + size)
Plastic sheeting, wraps, bags

Options
Potter's wheel
Rolling pins (commercial baker's
weight, if possible)
Jars (all kinds and sizes)
Lots of seemingly useless junk

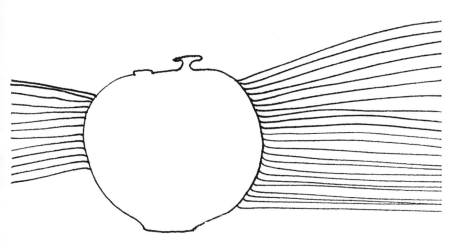

POTWORKS:
A FIRST BOOK OF CLAY

I

Kilns and Firing

Essentially, a kiln is a well-insulated box, dome, cylinder, cave, or hole, that saves and contains heat. If you are asking why start here, the answer is that without a kiln a pottery has no heart: nothing is transformed and nothing works. Before you build, buy or borrow a wheel, before you dig or mix your clay, think about your kiln. This may sound upside down and a little crazy to those of you who are involved with the wheel now, trying to become its master. However, if you are ready or need to pot on your own, try to consider your kiln as a center. All kinds of things radiate from your kiln: heat energy, atmospheric changes, space and power demands, cyclical imperatives, negative and good vibes. Your kiln will determine the technical limits of your pottery: its maturation temperature, the type of glazes, the dimensions and scale of your work.

Unfortunately, we don't all have choices open to us about kilns. Money and location determine a lot of things at first. Most beginning potters today are city potters, not of their choosing. City kilns present great and special problems. If you are going to pot in a densely populated city, it will be difficult to set up or use a natural-fuel kiln; not impossible, just difficult. If you locate in an industrially zoned neighborhood, can get a sizable loft with good, really good, ventilation and a potential flue or chimney exit, a solid floor, can find an obliging gas plumber or oil company, and an easily bribed fire (substitute buildings, police, utilities) inspector(s), you're set. Skip this whole chapter and go out and get Paul Soldner's pamphlet, *Kiln Construction*, the August, 1970 *Craft Horizons*, and if you have a lot of bread, Daniel Rhodes' *Kilns: Design, Construction and Operation*. They can tell you more about natural-fuel firing than I can. If you do build a fuel-fired kiln in a city pottery, make sure that you have a commodious space and don't have to be up against walls or ceilings. If your neighbors seem to be uptight about the black smoke, reduce at night after they've gone home to Babylon.

A natural-fuel kiln is powered by burning something. Through the burning process heat energy is released. The potter tries to save in his kiln as much of that released heat energy as possible. In that way he increases the temperature inside his kiln.

An electric kiln burns nothing. There is no combustion proper. Electric kilns get hot through the production of heat energy in an entirely different manner from combustion. Heat is generated by the resistance of coiled metal wires to the charge run through them. This heat is radiated into the kiln and, hopefully, saved by good kiln insulation. The bigger the charge, the more energy released. The more efficient the insulation, the greater the temperature potential of the kiln. Once a certain level of intensity is reached in an electric kiln, some burning takes place. Organic matter in the kiln or in the clay burns when the atmosphere reaches a high enough temperature. This combustion doesn't release enough energy to "fire" your kiln (increase its temperature).

Potters will tell you that the difference between electric and natural-fuel firing is basically the difference between an oxidizing and a reducing fire. A reducing fire is one that is starved for oxygen. This situation arises when the potter cuts back his kiln's air supply during the firing or when he greatly increases the fuel input (the carbon). The oxygen decrease forces the excess carbon in the kiln atmosphere to hunt for a supply of oxygen. The carbon finds its needed oxygen in the metallic oxides present in the clays and glazes of the wares. The carbon snatches up whatever oxygen molecules it can get and in this way *reduces* the metallic oxides to their base metals. The metallic oxides yield their oxygen to the combustion process. Carbon robbing the oxides makes glazes and clays take on colors characteristic of the metals, not their oxides. An example is the celadon family of glazes where red iron oxide has been used as a colorant and yet the glazes come out of the reducing fire as cool gray-greens or even bluish, and not rusty brown or tan.

During an oxidizing fire, oxygen combines with carbon to produce carbon dioxide. This reaction is known as burning or combustion. An oxidizing fire is characterized by complete combustion of the available carbon (fuel). A reducing fire cannot utilize the available carbon fully because of the decreased oxygen supply. The difference is made physically clear: reducing kilns have smoky-looking fires (lots of extra carbon), oxidizing fires burn comparatively clear and bright.

Electric kilns are always described as having an oxidizing atmosphere. The oxygen in an electric kiln is always sufficient for the minimal burning that takes place because there is no constant carbon (fuel) input taking place during an electric firing. The heat increase is achieved by resistance, radiation, and conduction. I don't even like to think of electric kilns in relation to "oxidizing" or "reducing" atmospheres. An electric kiln firing is a more neutral process of generating heat energy than the highly complex, chemically busy, and interactive burning of natural fuels to heat kilns. Since it is a more inert atmosphere, electric firing tends to yield more inert-looking glazes. With a lot of work you can counteract this tendency. In a sense there's no fire at all in electric firing but we all talk of electric firing and the English even call electric heating appliances "fires," so I'm staying with the general usage in this text. Just try to keep in mind that where there is smoke there is fire, but where there is heat there is not necessarily burning, in the chemical sense.

Electric kilns are portable, small-scaled, dependable, and boring, but don't let the last stop you. In recent years new insulating material has been developed that makes it possible to have a lightweight, seven-to-nine-cubic-foot kiln that fires up to stoneware temperatures, that can be moved, taken apart, added on to, and turned off automatically, if necessary. Such kilns are usually eight-to-ten-sided, top-loading, thin-walled (new types of insulating brick are used), and the novice's best friend.

Despite what all the greatest potters say and what all the best authorities write, you can make excellent pots and glaze them beautifully using electric power. It takes only about five times more glaze research to produce interesting, various, and inviting glazes with electricity than it does with a kiln that burns something, i.e., gas, oil, coal, wood. The reason for this extra work is described above: the chemically less active atmosphere that exists in the electric powered firing. Don't be depressed by the obvious bias demonstrated by Rhodes, Leach, Nelson, et al., in favor of natural-fuel firing (reducing atmosphere) at high temperatures. Just because industry makes lousy, boring glazes with electric power does not mean you have to do likewise. Industry manages to make some banal glazes with gas too.

First, get to know the difference between a good glaze

and an uninviting one. Good glazes invite handling, possess color depth and richness, and can't be verbally described. They also conform to certain basic technical requirements: complete fusion, hardness, well-fitted to the underlying clay body of the pottery. Go look at a lot of pots: all different kinds of pots. Clay does all kinds of things. Take a look at: agitated, wildly decorative Persian pots, Valencian lusterware, Sung celadons, Chün pots, Korean inlaid wares, as many Japanese pots as you can get to, Rhenish salt jugs, English slipware, and twentieth-century American stoneware.

If you have to fire with electricity, do the things that electricity does best: intense, flat, low-fire enamels, brilliant low-fire lead and alkaline glazing, Egyptian paste, middle-range stoneware fired from cone 4 to cone 7. High-fire stoneware is costly to produce in small electric kilns. Taking your kiln up to cone 8 or 9 with electricity costs a great deal (especially in an expensive energy city like New York), is hard on the elements, and still does not yield certain glazes characteristic of the high-fire range, reduced copper reds or celadons. If your kiln has Kanthal elements and you wish to make a more durable ware than earthenware, make stoneware at cone 4 to cone 7. This is also comparatively unexplored territory. Reams have been written on the extremes: high-fired stoneware and porcelain, and low-fired pottery, but there is a huge in-between range that is relatively unexplored by studio potters.

Your electric kiln does not reach the target temperature by burning something constantly for the resultant heat energy. As I have said, the energy release stems from the resistance of coiled metal wires. The temperature climb results from resistance, radiation, and conduction; heat energy being saved and contained in your well-insulated kiln chamber. The metal wire coils must be capable of withstanding unusually high heats. Nichrome alloy elements will go to earthenware temperature. A kiln must be equipped with Kanthal elements to fire to stoneware temperatures. Globars also withstand high heats.

Protect your elements. Elements that constantly have crap on them—glaze drippings, clay fragments, kiln wash, or anything else that is alien—will be short-lived. Most recently manufactured electric kilns have some element protection built in to them. The elements are either set in a deeply recessed groove or are placed into protective holders set into the walls. I prefer the generalized groove to the holders. Sometimes the holders and elements get old and fused together after an accident or two. This makes for more difficult element replacement. Look for such protective features if you're buying a kiln. When firing, protect the elements by not setting ware too close to the walls of the kiln, by not introducing carbonaceous matter in any great quantity into the kiln, by using glazes that do not vaporize or run madly during your firings, and by reducing the prospects of steam explosions by putting only very dry (bone-dry) ware in the kiln and firing very slowly in the initial stages.

Deformation and sagging of element coils into the kiln chamber can be remedied somewhat by shoving them back into place and securing them with Kanthal pins. Push the coils back with a light touch, since they are often brittle in their old age. This kind of repair can usually be avoided by paying attention to the protection points listed above. But in case you inherit a free kiln with sagging elements, try to reposition them and pin them back before any extensive firing.

Even with the most careful attention and forethought, elements die. Kiln elements have a natural lifetime. They wear out. Pin down the maker of your kiln on the question of what kind and quality elements went into the making of your kiln. Remember when stacking the kiln to be generous to the elements. Don't expect one ring of coils to bear the strain of heating a densely loaded shelf of low pieces. Engage at least two coil rows per level of ware. It doesn't look space-saving when you're loading, but it consumes less electrical energy in the end and prolongs the elements' lives.

The insulating brick used to make the walls, floors, lids, or doors of electric kilns is probably a good quality, high-temperature-rated brick, no matter what brand of kiln you buy or get hold of. Note that these soft insulating bricks are extremely fragile. They chip and crack easily. There are mending cements available for repairs. Sometimes a paste of fireclay and grog can be used for repairing chips and cracks. There are cements that adhere, repair, add insulating value, and help heat radiation by adding to the light-colored brick's reflection capacity a glossy reflecting layer. Such cements are hair-raisingly expensive, priced around twenty-five dollars a gallon. If, however, you've come into a kiln that seems to need a huge amount of brick repair in the chamber, look into using a quart of one of these cements. They'll probably pay for themselves over a long period of firing.

The design of lids, doors, and floors varies greatly in quality. These sections show firing fatigue long before the walls, in most cases. There are kilns on the market that have replaceable lids and floors. Sometimes replacing a damaged floor can salvage an entire kiln. If you are buying a kiln, keep such features in mind. Kilns with doors—that is, front-loaders—cost more. It costs more money and labor to hang a door on a kiln because the structure must be reinforced to bear the weight of the door. Front-loaders do not have replaceable floors or lids. Most people buy a front-loading kiln because they feel that stacking the kiln is easier. I disagree on this point and in general prefer top-loading electric kilns to front-loading electric kilns.

Front-loaders are more costly, tend to have cool spots at the doors, and fire unevenly due to the square shape. Box-shaped kilns seem to me to have more firing unevennesses, hot and cold spots, than the new quasi-round kilns. In addition, novices seem to learn to stack more consciously and more easily with a top-loader. They can see down onto the shelves and see directly whether or not pieces are touching each other. So, don't go out of your way for a door.

Many city agencies will take an interest in your operations. Fire and buildings inspectors are sure to drop in after your kiln is installed. They seem to materialize out of nowhere, considering that you usually have not gone out of your way to tell them what you are about. They are probably alerted by your local utilities company. If your kiln has some kind of metal jacket, even if it is as thin as a sheet of foil, it makes inspectors feel better. These steel jackets don't add any heat retention value, but do seem to give inspectors the impression that "fire" will be contained. A large, noticeable bucket of sand, or grog, standing around near your kiln will also make inspectors feel more secure.

The only thing you really need for secure operations is an absolutely unquestionable heavy wiring job. This is going to cost you a fortune if there are no heavy-duty power lines running to your chosen kiln location. Most utility companies will not run a 220 volt line to you until you come up with a duly *licensed electrical contractor* to run a heavy-duty cable from the electric company's meter to your kiln. Con Ed may feel good that your electrician is licensed but make sure he has installed kilns before. You must be really careful about who does your wiring. There are a lot of electricians floating around who economize in the wrong places and don't know anything about kilns and who pay no attention to your kiln company's suggestions, wiring diagrams, etc. This kind of electrician will screw your whole operation. If you already have a 220-volt capacity in your building, you may be able to wire the kiln yourself, get a capable moonlighter, or someone you feel really understands electricity and kilns. If the heavy-duty power has to be brought to the building for the first time, the installation may cost as much as the kiln. At this writing, a new installation running only to a ground-floor site, in New York City, that employs a licensed contractor, that is in a relatively near position to the building's electrical basement (meters), will start somewhere around $325 and go up and up depending on where you are in terms of neighborhood and physical location in your chosen building.

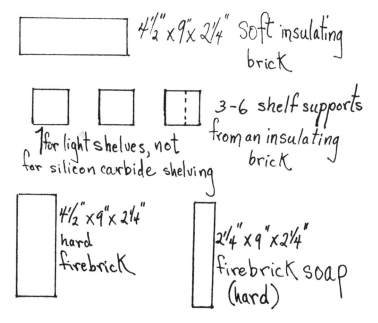

$4\frac{1}{2}'' \times 9'' \times 2\frac{1}{4}''$ Soft insulating brick

3–6 shelf supports from an insulating brick

for light shelves, not for silicon carbide shelving

$4\frac{1}{2}'' \times 9'' \times 2\frac{1}{4}''$ hard firebrick

$2\frac{1}{4}'' \times 9'' \times 2\frac{1}{4}''$ firebrick soap (hard)

Kiln furniture consists of *shelves* and *supports*. These are the basics. Nothing else is essential. Don't spend for fancy items such as spurs, stars, stilts, or points. The one extraordinary piece you may want or need at some later time is a tile or plate setter, if you get into these things regularly.

All kinds of posts, supports, or columns are available. The new flexible, small, interlocking posts are very convenient and not too expensive. Beware of your local hobby supplier. He'll be glad to sell you so-called high-temperature kiln furniture that doesn't really make it. If you're not sure of your source, make your own supports out of high-temperature, soft, insulating brick. Insulating brick can be cut with a hand saw into many useful and various heights.

If you can locate some *soaps*, you're in luck. Soaps are hard firebricks that are one half a normal firebrick, measuring 9 inches (like a firebrick in height) but only 2½ inches in width and thickness. Soaps make the sturdiest and longest lasting supports for shelves that accommodate an 8- or 9-inch level of pots. The soaps may be stacked one atop the other for a sturdy 18-inch supportive column, when firing really high pieces. If you consistently work large, they are worth going out of your way to find. Usually, you can get them only at a large refractories yard. When using soft brick supports make sure to use extra supports whenever the weight on a level is unusual. This precaution isn't necessary when utilizing soaps.

Shelves are thin, extended, flat refractory shapes. The use of shelves enables the potter to load the kiln evenly and efficiently.

Since shelves are rather thin refractories, they don't wear well. After many firings they sag or warp. Some cheap shelves crack easily. Some expensive shelving, such as high-temperature silicon carbide shelves, tends to be brittle by nature. You must try to handle your shelves in the most conscious and generous manner. They are very expensive to replace. Store shelves out of major traffic aisles in the pottery, stacked in a careful, thought-out fashion, when not in use in the kiln.

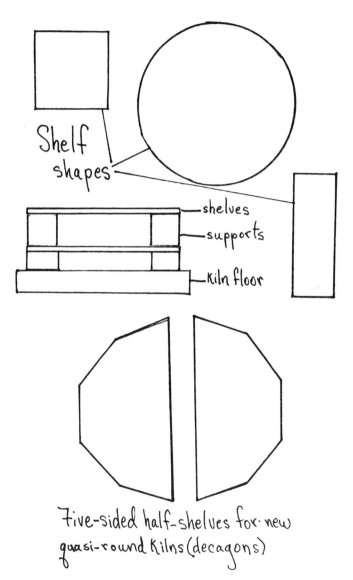

Shelf shapes

shelves
supports
Kiln floor

Five-sided half-shelves for new quasi-round Kilns (decagons)

BISCUITS

Biscuit firing or bisqueing are terms for a first firing of clay. Usually (there are exceptions), a bisque firing yields porous, immature, unglazed pottery that won't hold water. Why do it? Some people don't.* However, there are positive reasons for bisque firing. It drives off the chemically combined water that is in your seemingly bone-dry greenware. After bisque firing, the clay can never again be physically broken down and reconditioned by soaking in water for reuse. Bisqued ware is less fragile and therefore less difficult to handle than dry greenware. Pots are more easily carried and handled during glazing if they have been bisqued. The decrease in fragility also allows for storage, if the need arises. This may not seem important at first. You may be glazing directly after every bisque kiln. But there do come times in the potter's life when it becomes necessary to store ware, and that's much more easily done in the biscuit state than in the green state. You can pile one piece into the next (with some margin of care), wrap it all up to prevent dust accumulation, and stick it out of the way while you: move, formulate new glazes, produce more heavily, teach, rethink your involvement, or whatever else has necessitated the change in pace.

In general, it is easier to glaze, decorate, and physically

---

* Some potters skip the first firing. They do this by adjusting their glazes to attain good results in a single firing or by employing firing processes that eliminate a first firing to a low temperature (such as salt-glaze firing, where the potter fires his green pots up to their final maturation point in one shot). Common industrial practice reverses the studio stoneware procedure by firing to the higher temperature initially (and calling it the "bisque firing"), and then doing a second firing at a lower temperature, which is actually a glaze firing. This practice substantially reduces handling and accident losses. As I've stated in the wordlist, I use the term bisque in this text to refer to a first firing to a low temperature.

handle bisque than greenware. Knobs, handles, and other protruding parts of pots are less likely to break and split away once things are bisqued. And of course the porous, open bisque absorbs glazes rapidly and easily.

STACKING A BISQUE KILN

Loading or *stacking* a bisque kiln is a relatively simple operation. Pieces may touch each other, since there is no glaze on them. Unglazed pieces cannot fuse together. Small pieces may be placed inside larger ones and the latter placed in still larger ones. Load densely and distribute your ware evenly. Try not to place pieces in unsupported positions or in positions that create tense spots around rims or other delicate parts of your pots. Place lids in their pots so that both lid and pot shrink, warp, or go through the same changes together. Be very careful to support plaques, plates and other pieces characterized by extension. Handles, spouts, and other protuberances should not hang over the shelving; they may distort during the firing.

It's easier to stack if you have shelves or a table near the kiln. A used service cart on wheels will do if you have no room near the kiln for a more permanent fixture. Group all your green pieces on the table according to height. On the basis of these different height groupings, calculate roughly how many levels you will need and whether the levels will be for low or high or medium pieces. Allow for the thickness of each level of shelves (about ½ inch per shelf). This rough preliminary surveying and arranging will save lots of time during the stacking proper. It cuts out trips back and forth and the possible breakage that arises from excessive or rushed handling. Try to find a carpenter's level that just fits the span of your kiln's chamber. It has a ruler along one edge and can be used to measure heights and diameters closely. It doesn't warp. It is useful as a spanner rod, to check on whether pieces are within the height limits of their shelves. A level is the most convenient tool to have around when loading. Height checking looks like this:

Using a carpenter's level for height checks

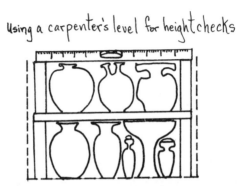

The first thing you put down on the floor of your kiln is not a pot. Put your support posts down first so that you can see exactly what space remains to be filled with pots. For square kilns I've found a tri-pointed support system most space-saving. You want the supports to give adequate, even support but not to take up too much space. In a square kiln the supports for the next shelf would look like this:

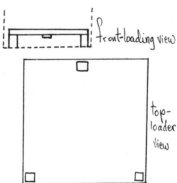

front-loading view

top-loader view

In a quasi-round kiln:

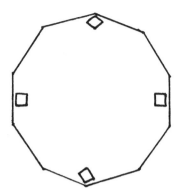

The columns must support the next level in a stable and sufficient way. Test for the stability of your arrangement by spreading the fingers of one hand and placing it, all fingers open and spanning the shelf as widely as possible, on the shelf and then jiggling the shelf. If the shelf (or shelves) don't wobble noticeably, the support is suitable. Go on to loading pots. If the shelf is shaky, you probably need to reposition the columns or add another support. More pillars yield more stability, but leave room for some pots.

Be generous in height allowance between shelves. Theoretically, it is all right to allow the top of a piece to touch the shelf above in a bisque firing because it won't fuse to the shelf. In practice, though, I've found that this doesn't allow any breathing room to the pot during the stage of the firing when it is most expanded. Hairline cracks and distortions in the rim result in the pieces if they have no room to expand. So allow the pots space above them as well as around them. It helps proper heat circulation too. As you become less nervous about stacking and more proficient, you can get to loading very tight bisque kilns. In the beginning it's better to waste some space than lose pots. Aim toward tight, evenly stacked kilns as a goal. You will be using your kiln and the electricity more efficiently when you reach that goal.

The visible gauge you need, to know where your firing is at, is a series of *pyrometric cones*. Usually, three cones are set up in a pat of clay:

red clay cones are for bisque and other low-temperature firings

jab in many air holes or use lots of grog in the clay for cone pats, prevents cracking

white clay cones are for high-temperature firings

The first cone is one that corresponds to a gradation *below* your target temperature. When it bends it announces that you're very near your desired goal temperature. The second cone is the target cone. When it bends all the way down, turn off. In some cases potters don't turn off at this point. They stop the temperature increase but maintain the fuel or power input to *soak* the entire kiln in an even, thorough heat. Don't allow the last cone to lay itself out flat. If the last cone in the series bends totally, you will have achieved an *overfiring*. You will have shot beyond your mark. In a bisque firing this is not a great calamity, if it's only a cone's difference. Your fired bisque will probably still be porous enough to suck up glazes. In a glaze firing an *overfiring* is much more serious. After the bisque firing, the cone pat should look something like this:

after firing

In any event, the main point to remember at this stacking stage is to place your cone pat in front of your peephole as soon as stacking has reached the level of your kiln's peephole. Place your support posts, then your cone pat, then your pots. Trying to find a space for the cone pat after the shelf is loaded with pots is a nuisance. Beginners also have a tendency to forget altogether to put the cones in. Don't panic if you've managed to do just that. Turn the kiln off when it reaches a light, bright, cherry color.

If you've had the chance to fire a kiln fifty times or so you can probably judge temperatures inside the kiln on the basis of the chamber's visible color. Some potters are very blithe in their recommendations to beginners on this matter. It is relatively easy to use color as a gauge in bisque firing. You have to be very experienced to do glaze firings on the basis of color gauging only. Don't kid yourself. It may seem more direct, natural, and appealing than cone pats. It's reliable only after long years of firing experience.

The bisque temperature your pots need will vary with the particular clay you are using and with your preferences. You may like a really soft, absorbent bisque for particular glazes. If your glazing tends toward a thin use of glaze, you might not want too much absorbency. You might like a harder bisque because you store it a lot and want it less fragile. You may skip bisqueing altogether at some point. Your glazes would have to be adjusted especially for that purpose.

If your clay matures in the cone 4 to cone 7 range, you will probably bisque somewhere between cone 09 and cone 07. If you glaze fire at the cone 8 to cone 10 range you may prefer to bisque somewhere between cone 08 and cone 06. For low-fire glazing at cone 04, you can use cone 010 or cone 09 as a bisque target temperature. These are rough guides and you should feel free to change your bisque temperature if glazes are not being absorbed properly upon application or if you are having many breakage incidents due to softness. Try to buy your cones wholesale, in bulk, directly from the Orton Foundation. The address for the Orton Foundation is in the suppliers list at the end of the book.

Wrap your pieces up well after the bisque firing, if you are not going to glaze them immediately. A layer of dust makes for glazing problems. Prevent it. You can and must wash the ware before glazing if it's been standing around awhile. The washing and drying of bisque can be minimized by protected storage.

FIRING IT

An electric-powered bisque firing consists of bringing your kiln up to temperature as slowly as possible. Actually the slowness must be only in the initial stages. The first few hours of heat must be very gradual or you will get steam explosions. You want to drive off the chemically combined water in this firing but not so fast as to agitate the molecules into panicky escapes from the clay. If a lot of steam wants to escape fast it will .simply blow out of the vessel and split it. Going up too fast and coming down too rapidly are the only problems in firing a bisque kiln with electricity. Most of the little electric kilns just go up too fast. They don't have separate switches for each set of coil elements. Start this kind of kiln with an open door or lid and keep the peephole open if you can. Add an hour or two for this kind of preheating to the firing cycle suggested by your kiln manufacturer. If you have a number of switches on your kiln you can reduce the open-door time to an hour, but keep the kiln on the lowest setting for another hour. Don't jump from low to high. Allow for a nice rounded medium period. In any kiln over seven cubic feet, this preheating should go on for a few hours. The specific lengths of time for each setting must vary greatly. Density of load and overall size and shape make for a lot of variation. Don't be surprised at your kiln taking two or three hours longer to make temperature on occasion. You probably had an unusually tight stacking. Advance to high and keep a steady eye on your cones. Turn off when your target cone (middle of the three) is down all the way.

On cracking kilns—wait. You know what is said: don't just do something, stand there. The rule of thumb is to wait out a time period equal to the time it took to fire the kiln to temperature. Many electric kilns cool too rapidly. There are several danger points in the cooling down period. They should be passed slowly. If you hear breakage or get cracks that you think take place during the cooling, try a protective wrapping for the next firing. Wrap your kiln in a blanket of some insulating material so that you slow down the cooling. Cracking a kiln is just that: opening it a crack. Crack it. Then wait some more. Prop up the lid or door and open the peephole(s). Wait some more. Open the door or lid all the way and wait again. Some people wait until they can handle the fired pots with their bare hands. Some potters unload the kiln using mitts. Some people burn themselves. Do what is best for your pots. Don't subject them to the shock of the cold outside world until they're cool. Just get used to waiting.

The insulating material in the walls of your kiln is supposed to protect your pots from the outside world. If you're getting rapid cooling all the time, and the wrapping doesn't help, check your kiln's situation. If you've got a serviceable but fatigued old kiln, set it up out of the way of sudden drafts. A shop door opened on a windy, 15° day can let in a shock of cold air. Build a buffer wall if you can't move the kiln.

THE GLAZE KILN

There is a big point to keep constantly in mind when stacking a glaze kiln; and it is the major difference between bisque and glaze stacking. Pieces must not touch each other in the stacked glaze kiln. They will come out of the kiln fused together, if you allow them to nestle up close to one another. This no-touch rule goes for all pots, kiln furniture, tops and bottoms of pieces in relation to shelves, lids in relation to flanges, cone pats, everything in the kiln. When your cones lean over at target temperature they need space or they'll attach to anything nearby. You can always chisel, hammer, or grind pieces apart but you risk damaging the pieces in the separation process, to say nothing of what your pieces may look like with the vestiges of thoughtlessness.

And so we arrive at *dry-footing*. Most authors mention dry-footing. They tell you to do it to pieces that are to go into a glaze kiln. Most simply, it means to wipe off all glaze from the bottom of the piece. If you leave the bottom glazed, your piece will exit from the kiln permanently glued to its shelf. Molten glass makes a nearly unbeatable adhesive. You won't be able to separate shelf and pot. Even small dots of glaze at a few strategic bottom points can produce this loving attachment.

If you are producing pottery in some quantity, you will save time and have more uniform results by dry-footing with wax. Blocks of paraffin can be melted in a pan over a hot plate. When the paraffin has melted to a clear, liquid state, hold your pots by the rim and dip the foot, one at a time, into the hot wax. Coating with wax is done before you begin glazing operations. After the wax is applied, upend the pieces and allow them to dry on their rims. When the wax is dry you can go ahead and dip or pour on your glazes and watch the glaze run off the waxed bottoms. This technique is a *resist* process. The waxed areas resist absorbing the glaze. The part of the pot under the wax absorbs no glaze and is thus "dry-footed." A variation of this process is used for decorative purposes and is called wax-resist decoration.

Liquid wax emulsions are also available. These can be thinned a bit with water and pieces dipped in the stuff. Bottoms may also be painted with these emulsions. Painting the feet takes more time than dipping but it saves on the emulsions and is still less time-consuming than wiping glazed bottoms with wet sponges. The emulsions are very useful in decorating pots with glaze. Wax-resist painted decoration is facilitated by the use of emulsions.

The waxes burn out during firing. Paraffin stinks when it burns out in any quantity. The emulsions seem to burn out with less stench and fewer visible fumes. The thinner you apply paraffin or wax emulsions, the less organic stuff there is to burn out. Keep this in mind while dry-footing with wax. I've frequently dry-footed entire kiln loads of ware with wax and not damaged the elements. If you leave the door or lid open until dull red heat is achieved the carbon burns off and exits without impairing the elements.

If you don't need to or don't want to use wax, be very careful to wipe off glaze thoroughly from the bottoms, using a damp sponge. Usually you must wipe the glaze off after the whole piece has dried. If the glaze on the piece is still wet when you dry-foot, you wind up picking up spots of damp glaze on your fingertips when you set the pot down. This results in naked, unglazed spots on the fired, finished pot. These bald spots don't particularly bother me, but sometimes get to be too offensive. Often students dust off a great deal of glaze while dry-footing and are aghast at the unglazed areas revealed after firing.

Another basic means of avoiding pots getting stuck to shelves is to use kiln wash. Kiln wash is not an arcane specialty of your local supplier. It is only equal parts, by weight, of *kaolin* (china clay, any china clay will do) and *flint* (potter's silica), mixed with enough water to make a creamy paint. Kaolin and flint are both super-refractory. Without a flux they'll never fuse at your temperatures. Therefore, they make a perfect protective wash.

I cover only floors and shelves with kiln wash. Pass the kaolin and flint mixture (wet) through your glaze sieve a couple of times. Sieving it homogenizes the mixture. Add some more water if the mix is too thick. Paint it on floors and shelves. Two thin coats is enough to protect them. If a glaze should run off or you overfire, your pots can usually be separated from the shelves. Even if chaos has been created in the kiln, it's usually possible to salvage pots, shelves and all. Just chip at the mess carefully and patiently. Clean off the shelves and rewash them. Do this after each glaze firing and your shelves will always be ready for the next stacking. Some people apply kiln wash to the side walls, doors, lids, etc., usually for better heat reflection and protection. On the whole, I think this is unnecessary and runs the risk of a novice painting up his elements with kiln wash; not too healthy for the elements.

Kiln wash prevents pots from adhering to shelves by creating a buffer zone between pieces and shelves. Should you have some kind of glaze kiln accident and your pots come away from their shelves with wash and glaze drips at the feet, it can be ground down with a silicon carbide grinding wheel. The major way to avoid dependence on the grinding wheel for finished feet is to glaze carefully and fire attentively. A good layering of wash not only helps in such crises, it also extends the lifetime of your shelves. Since the shelves are always an expensive replacement problem, you've got to develop an overprotective attitude toward them. Constant firing chaos will cost you more in replacements for shelves and elements than you would expect.

Pots expand during firing and will stick to the shelves above if their tops have been allowed to touch during the loading. Again, be generous; at least a half an inch of air space should be above the tops of your pots. Check this by using a spanner rod as described above in the bisque stacking section. In a top-loading situation it is easy to be visually tricked by the appearances of similar height pots. Make sure not to use a warped or sagging rod when you height check. In a front-loading kiln make sure you check out the far back points. This height-checking business is much more crucial for a glaze kiln stacking than for bisque stacking. You may damage a piece or two in a bisque loading by allowing them to touch the next shelf above. In a glaze kiln those pieces will not only stick fused to the shelf (and come out damaged), they'll screw up the shelves.

In general, leave more room around pieces when stacking a glaze kiln; an inch if you're new at it. If your glazes are all new and tests, be even more generous. Unknowns can do all kinds of weird things in a glaze firing. You can get down to quarter-inch or eighth-of-an-inch separations when you're proficient at stacking and when you know the behavior of your glazes well. Some circulation space allowance helps to make for even firings. Run your fingers under rims that hang over smaller pieces. It is space-saving to arrange some little things under broad overhangs but it doesn't save in the end if the little things are stuck to the larger piece.

Remember that glazes bubble, expand, run, at times vola-tize, or migrate a bit. Even loading is better than dense cramming when stacking a glaze kiln. Avoid the tempta-tion of getting everything you've readied into the firing at hand. If it looks really crowded during loading it will be worse when the pots get hot and swell up to their heated maximums. Even stacking makes for more even heat and for fewer ghastly surprises at opening time.

You know you have hot and cold spots in your kiln when one old reliable glaze begins to look different because it's been on different pots in differing locations. The symptom: Glaze X turns out somewhat underfired-looking, unusually mat or dry surfaced on one pot that was on the first level of your last glaze kiln, while its brother, stacked near the top of the kiln (same exact glaze), looks extremely glossy, the glaze even ran a bit and has collected in a drop near the foot of the pot. If you think that your glaze application was even and you know both pots were glazed with the same batch of glaze, start looking closely at the rest of your wares. Was everything from that top shelf tending toward glossiness or unusual runniness? If it looks that way, be sure to place cone pats on *each shelf* during your next glaze stacking. Sprinkling cone pats around the kiln, in addition to using the regular one at the peephole, will give you some data to analyze. If there is little difference among the various cone pats after your next glaze firing, say a half cone's difference, there's probably nothing to worry about. If the third cone is flattened out on some of the pats, it means it was much hotter in those spots. Adjust your glazes for a wider firing range, if your kiln is generally behaving this way. Check your elements by opening your kiln and turning on each element, a switch at a time. If you don't have several switches, just wait to see if they all come on. Unevennesses in electric kilns are often a sign of elements ending their natural lives. If one has died, replace it. If your hot spots seem to be at the top of the kiln (and your elements seem fine), and you have a peephole up near the top of the kiln, open it during the firing. Let some of that rising, hot air out. It may work to cool the top shelf down to the temperature of the rest of the kiln. Stack with your hot and cold spots in mind if you are not able to work out some evening-out rituals. Put glossy glazed pieces in your cooler kiln spots and mat glazed pieces in the warmer ones. Dry-foot high on pieces going into hotter parts of the kiln. Accepting your kiln's individuality takes some adaptation on your part.

Now that you have some ideas about what a kiln is and how it works, you can practice stacking a kiln. All the mechanical movements will become second nature with repeated firings. Control of the firing is very important in the creation of good pots.

Getting back to the idea of your kiln being a focus of attention, I have some general suggestions. Try to cultivate the idea of the kiln being a precious center, rather than the idea of your individual pots being the precious center. By evolving a healthy respect for your "fire" you'll come to understand it. In this way, the kiln will come to serve at the creation of your better pots. Otherwise, the pots always seem fine before firing and somehow "messed up" after the glaze kiln is unloaded. It seems the fault of the firing. Some potters even get into thinking of the firing as an antagonistic element in the overall process. I think you can get the fire working for you and your pots by giving it its due early in your own growth.

Attempt to really understand the technical behavior of your particular kiln. Books are too general. They can't possibly deal with the thousands of variables to be found in differing kilns, within the limits of a hundred pages or so. When you do turn to a book for help, concentrate on the theoretic presented, not the details. The specific details may be irrelevant for your particular kiln. Collect information on specifics from your kiln manufacturer, fuel and power companies, manufacturers of refractory products, concerns that deal with high-temperature metal alloys, electricians, plumbers, and utilities personnel, and other potters and kiln-builders. We have no organic living tradition through which we could come to specific information, as did generations of Chinese or Japanese potters, so we have to go the more contrived path of purposely collecting other people's experiences.

If you are potting intensively now, but are not handling the firing aspects, take time out from making things and hang out when your master fires his kilns. Get some experience of what is involved in firing, if the opportunity exists, before you find yourself in a situation where you have to fire your pots yourself and don't know what to do first.

Tune in on other potters when you hear them rapping about firing. Your memory will store all that secondhand experience up for you, toward the day when you'll need it.

In time, the fire will perform the final mysteries of transformation for you.

A special firing booklist:

Colson, Frank. "Workshop: Kiln Building with Space Age Materials," *Craft Horizons*, August, 1970, pp. 46–48.

Leach, Bernard. *A Potter's Book*. New York: Transatlantic Arts, 1948.

Nelson, Glenn C. *Ceramics*. New York: Holt, Rinehart and Winston, 1966.

Norton, F. H. *Ceramics for the Artist Potter*. Cambridge, Mass.: Addison-Wesley, 1956.

————. *Elements of Ceramics*. Cambridge, Mass.: Addison-Wesley, 1952.

————. *Refractories*. New York: McGraw-Hill, 1949.

Rhodes, Daniel. *Kilns; Design, Construction and Operation*. Philadelphia, Pa., Chilton, 1968.

Riegger, Hal. *Raku*. New York: Van Nostrand, 1970.

Soldner, Paul. *Kiln Construction*. New York: American Craftsmen's Council, 1965.

FIRING LOG   date...............

Turn on time ......

Preheat duration............
    (single burner or door [lid] open.)

Turn to medium...........
    or burner adjustments...........times......

Turn to high ....
Turn off..........   Total time........
Comments, additions:

II

The Primal Stuff

Potters work with clay. Essentially, we are involved in a magical transformation: the metamorphosis of spineless, sticky, muddy ooze into stony, hard, durable forms; forms possessed of color and tactile appeal. Independent forms that last, on their own, are not possible till you find a clay that is plastic; that holds its shape well during all the processes of formation and stages of drying, that reacts well with glazes, and that has an ultimate fired color that is warm and inviting to the touch. Prepared clay mixes sold by hobby suppliers rarely yield any of the above qualities.

Mix your own from the dry, pulverized air-floated clay that is sold through large distributors. To mix your own:

> 50% stoneware clay—Jordan, Monmouth, etc.
> 25% red clay—Ohio, Dalton, local surface clay
> 25% fireclay—A. P. Green Mexico-Missouri

The mix above is all clay. To mix a workable clay from this recipe you do not need very complicated equipment, machines, mills, or mixers. Take a very large plastic trash can and fill about two-thirds full with water. Before starting to mix, place it where you plan to keep your wet clay. You won't be able to move the mixture afterward. Add a cup of vinegar to the water in the plastic garbage can.

The vinegar will promote the growth of organisms needed for proper aging and plasticity. In a large basin, mix ten pounds of the above clays as follows: 5 lbs. stoneware clay, 2½ lbs. red clay, 2½ lbs. fireclay. Stir these dry ingredients thoroughly, and then gently add the dry, mixed clays into the water in the trash barrel. Sifting slowly, repeat mixed ten-pound additions until the water stops absorbing clay, or you run out, or you find the dusts in the air getting to intolerable levels.

Let your mixture stand, slake, and amalgamate; a couple of weeks if you are able to wait it out. Water will rise to the top of the barrel during this period. Some of it will evaporate. Siphon off the rest. Lay out the wet, wet clay on plaster, unfinished wood, or on a wood surface out in the sun; whatever surface is available to you for drying. When the clay is no longer gummy or sticky, and it comes away from the drying surface easily, it is ready to be wedged and prepared for use. Don't let your clay get too hard in this drying process. Your aim is to dry out excess water, not let the clay get to the stage of unplastic, unusable clods.

Clay must be prepared for use on the potter's wheel and for handbuilding. Wedging consists of cutting large amounts of clay into smaller pieces and reamalgamating them by forcefully throwing the pieces together. Spiral kneading consists of spiral turning movements that homogenize the clay and force out extra air in the process. This type of clay preparation is the most beneficial for clay to be used on the wheel. It demonstrably increases plasticity. On the whole, verbal descriptions of spiral kneading are not too helpful. See if you can find someone to show you how. If not, Bernard Leach says:

> The clay is turned slowly clock-wise, mainly by the left hand, the right hand taking a fresh hold after each pressure and release. The effect is to move the clay on the

outside towards the centre of the mass whence it works
out slowly to the circumference again.

A Potter's Book, pp. 51–52.

I knead thoroughly, even for handbuilding. It is at this
time that I wedge into the clay, *grog*. Grog is not a mysterious substance. It is a refractory clay, such as fireclay,
that has been pulverized after a firing, usually a firing
to a high temperature. Grog is added to clay for strength.
The major way it provides strength is by adding a pre-
fired element that will no longer shrink, or go through a
lot of changes during firings. Adding grog also creates
minute channels for air and gas passage during firing. In
other words, it opens up the clay body. In this way it
helps the clay pieces withstand the changes and stresses
of firing without collapse or explosion. Since it is stable
during the processes of formation, drying, and firing, it
contributes stability to clay wares throughout all the phases
of transformation. People who have used "sculpture clay"
are often under the impression that grog is added for
texture and often have the idea that it is somehow inherent
in "sculpture clay." Grog does add beautiful textures but
it is not an organic part of the clay mined from the earth;
it's a later, structural addition that you decide upon. You
can add grog as you mix your dry clays with water, if it
is a very fine particle-sized grog. Coarser grades tend to
settle down to the bottom of your mixing barrels because
of their weight. It will not help your clay body to have
an uneven distribution of grog, with a lightly grogged top
layer and a relatively heavily grogged lower layer. Add
such coarse types of grog during the wedging and kneading process. Adding at this point wears your wedging
table down but not too substantially. If you do a lot of
handbuilding, experiment with all kinds of grog. There is
a great variety of types and gradations available, includ-
ing colored variants. Specialized mesh sizes and colored

varieties are usually available only at the yards of large-scale refractories producers. Even though you may love the feel and look of grog, try not to go completely overboard. Keep the additions under 20 percent if you are planning to throw with the clay. A lot of grog in a throwing clay can abrade your fingers rapidly. If your hands are accustomed to it, you can throw with very heavily grogged clays. Adding grog to your clay body will influence the clay body's eventual maturation temperature. Adding grog allows you to fire your clay to a higher temperature. Since the grog is a pre-fired, highly refractory clay substance it will change your original clay mix to a more heat-resistant type of mixture. In this way you can extend the firing range of your clay in the direction of higher firing bodies. Generally, this is advantageous. Remain conscious of the overall tendency, however, if you are planning a grog addition of more than 20 percent. If you add a lot of grog you may wind up producing extremely open-bodied pots that have great textures but are so porous that they can't hold water. When you use your clay for sculptural pieces you should use more grog than you would for throwing. A very open body is desirable when building large, thick-walled structures.

The rough recipe given above is far from the beginning and end of clay body recipes. It is a very general recipe that is for use in the low stoneware firing range, cone 4 to cone 7. If you plan to fire to temperatures below 2000°F., add more red clay and decrease the fireclay and stoneware clay amounts. You may need 1 or 2 percent of a feldspar or talc in the body to make it mature at low temperatures, in addition to the red clay. If you wish to use this clay at the high stoneware range, from cone 8 to cone 10, increase the fireclay and decrease the red clay.

If you have no means of firing clay to high tempera-

tures, make sure that you use a low-fire clay body. Adjust
the recipe above or check out other sources. Low-fire
clays are available from hobby suppliers, sculpture supply
houses, brickyards, and from the ground. You can easily
mix a clay body from the dry state for low-temperature
firing. There are many recipes for low-fire bodies in Glenn
C. Nelson's *Ceramics*, the Rhodes books mentioned in the
booklist, and in back issues of *Ceramics Monthly*.

If you have been working at a school or center and
have used a clay you found pleasing, use that clay when
you work on your own. Track down the supply source or
locate the recipe and mix it in the plastic barrel fashion
described above. If the recipe is not basically clay or calls
for the mixing of five or six clays in small amounts, it isn't
a suitable recipe for the rough mixing method I've been
talking of above. It is too difficult to mix thoroughly and
disperse evenly a lot of different ingredients using the
garbage can method. If you plan to use a complicated
mix of clays, you must use a substantial mixing machine:
a large bread-dough mixer, a pug mill, or other such appliance. Don't kid yourself. If you don't have the bread
for this kind of equipment or aren't into such heavy production as to need tons of clay a year, make sure you work
out a simple clay body.

I suggest mixing your own clay to gain the experience.
It enables you to become intimate with your clay body
and its separate clay elements. All the verbal descriptions
of "tooth" or other such qualities won't mean a thing to
you until you have run some plain fireclay through your
fingers, wet and dry fireclay. Through the comparative,
experiential handling of clays you will find your way
among them. To use the books of Leach and Rhodes or
Cardew you'll need some of your own practical experience
of clay.

Another way of increasing your own clay experience

is to go out and dig it. You can usually find a way of digging your own clay without being an owner of country property. If you have access to a clay source, try it out. Dig out a sample batch of the clay, about ten pounds or so. Test it for plasticity by rolling coils and tying the coils, ring fashion, around your fingers. If the clay does not crack at the edges, it is plastic. Test for its firing range by drying it to your preferred workability state. Roll out some slabs and make a few small vessels. From the slabs, cut out some tiles. Measure the slab tiles before they dry, after they've dried to the bone-dry state, and then after bisque firing. These comparative measurements will tell you how much your clay shrinks. Measure the top and bottom diameters of the small pots you've made. Your first test firing should bring the pieces to your normal bisque temperature, somewhere in the cone 010 to cone 07 range. If the pieces show the qualities of bisque ware—porosity, softness, paleness of color, immaturity of sound when struck—assume the clay is bisqued. Put the pieces on unglazed flat tiles of your normal clay, and fire them up to your usual or projected glazing temperature. The small, flat tiles are a protective device. Should your unknown clay turn out to be a low-temperature clay, it may deform or begin to melt at a high firing temperature. In order to avoid a mess all over your kiln, the stuff is placed on a control tile. If you fire some unknown, low-temperature surface clay up to cone 8 or 9, it may turn out to be a natural slip clay glaze, not a clay body up at those temperatures. If you are in an area such as the region around Albany, N.Y., you may come up with a number of finds that might even include a natural stoneware clay, a potential slip glaze, as well as a usable surface clay. If your clay sample tests out encouragingly, you can dig more. Clean it of any unpleasant junk, sharp stones, etc., knead in some grog, and use it.

Once you are throwing in some quantity, proficiently and regularly, you will probably find digging and cleaning your own not a good alternative, economically. The digging and cleaning can become so time-consuming that the labor becomes too expensive. If the experiential value is becoming overwhelmed by economic pressures, it's probably more meaningful and energy-saving to mix your clay with the dry material commercially available. In time, it will be seen that digging clay can yield variable results. Digging a surface clay for a good, natural slip glaze is, I feel, almost always worth the labor. A few hundred pounds will yield a lot of glaze, whereas a few hundred pounds is not enough for a month's throwing clay, if you're producing, even in small quantity. The best information on digging and cleaning your own clay is found in the books of Bernard Leach and Michael Cardew. If you have found a good workable clay on your own land and it is a sizable deposit, tons preferably, and you are into using it, consult *Pioneer Pottery* and *A Potter's Book* before making a big decision.   **1734407**

Get to know the clay you work with intimately. Understand its tactile, textural, plastic nature; its technical properties: shrinkage rate, rate of absorption, tensile strength, chemical content and crystalline structure. The physical traits become apparent only through the experience of using clay. The technical grouping must be researched. Ask your clay supplier for data sheets on the specific clays you're buying and mixing. Such sheets contain a chemical analysis, and statistics on the technical properties listed above. The appendices in Rhodes' *Clay and Glazes for the Potter* contain information on how to go about testing your clays for this information. Understand that your specific kiln and firing temperature are very important determinants for such a feature as the exact percentage of shrinkage of a given clay. The technical stuff may bore you, but it will become more important to you as you go on, and especially if you get into heavy production. Knowing the technical potential of your clay helps you get better glaze behavior and better fitting lids, handles, and other utilitarian ware details. Of course, ancient potters didn't bother their heads about this stuff, but they had their fathers, and their fathers' fathers, around to tell them about the clays they were using. They worked with the same clays, the same kilns, and the same techniques for unbroken generations. None of us have come to pottery that way, in the West, for centuries. So badger your dealers for data. If such information is not readily available, get into Rhodes' *Clay and Glazes* soon. If he is going over your head, get some more practical experience and come back to all this when you are going on your own or getting into heavier production. The technical material is also important in troubleshooting. If you have no functional problems arising at the moment, move on to other areas of clay work and come back to the technical stuff when your natural curiosity compels you.

Finally, get to know your own preferences: how toothy or how smooth you like your clay, how long or short you tolerate it in throwing, how sticky or dry you like it, what colors you enjoy in a clay, whether you plan to hand-build or throw in the main, how crude or finished you like the finished surfaces of your pottery.

Try not to confuse wetness with workability, if you can help it. If your walls collapse a lot, your clay is probably too damp to work. Give it some more time to dry out. Beginners tend to blame themselves for everything that goes wrong. Sometimes it really is a problem with the clay. When you mix your clay with crude methods, give it plenty of drying time and lots of spiral kneading. If you are not really happy with your clay, change it before your head gets into a syndrome of endless little adjustments.

Take the problem that bothers you most, and attack it forcefully. Remember that you are dealing with a primal matter. If your clay doesn't satisfy you, it makes no sense to develop glazes for that clay, adjust your firing to it, or make any other changes around the body. Change your body.

Color is easily changed. Moving from electric to natural-fuel firing usually produces a favorable color change. This will be discussed later on. The basic way of changing clay color is to add or remove * iron or other coloring oxides. If your clay is buff to a boring degree, add any of the following clays: Barnard, Dalton, Cedar Heights Red. These are all heavy iron-bearing clays. Their addition to the clay body will change your clay color substantially in the direction of warm beige, tan, red, red-brown, depending upon the amount added. Colored, low-fire clays such as these can be added to a body in larger amounts than straight coloring oxides. Clay additions can start around 10 percent. If you are mixing the body suggested at the beginning of this chapter, add the new clay to the ten-pound mixes, before sifting the ten-pound units into the water.

You can experiment and change the ratios around, but keep your firing temperature before you. Adding low-fire clays is equal to adding flux to your clay body; too much will make your clay mature at a substantially lower temperature than it usually matures at.

Cheap grades of red iron oxide and manganese dioxide are available and are good color additions. Start with small

---

* I discuss changing the clay body color by adding colorants, but color change is often accomplished by moving in the opposite direction; that is, by removing colorant oxides from clays to make them whiter firing. Changes based on the removal of colorant oxides (particularly iron oxides) are most often the concern of industrial producers rather than studio potters. Color uniformity and predictability are deemed more essential in mass production operations than in studio-scale potting.

additions of the oxides, for they are strong fluxes and can lower your clay's maturation temperature radically if added in large quantities. About 1 or 2 percent is enough to produce noticeable color variation. If you add oxides to the clay recipe we started out with, mix a tablespoon of the oxide in with each ten-pound clay unit. This will distribute your total pound (or two) of oxide throughout the barrel of clay. In this way you can get a fairly even color throughout. When adding coloring oxides, start small. Sometimes too much red iron oxide in a clay will make it very slick for throwing. A sticky quality and heavy surface slick are indications of too much red iron oxide or heavy iron clay in the clay body. Some people enjoy clay of this very plastic feel.

There are good, industrially prepared body stains that are commercially available, but they are always expensive.

When experimenting with a new clay, or starting to change your current one, keep records. Take care to mark all test pots or tiles and to keep correlated notes or cards for each piece. Your system needn't be complicated, just systematic. Always mix test-sized batches when experimenting. I've found ten-pound amounts to be economical and still representative of a mixture's behavior. Try to test your planned variations around the same time, so that the testing stage doesn't go on and on.

Plasticity and strength are more difficult factors to resolve than achieving a satisfactory color. My basic approach has been to depend heavily on a locally available stoneware clay for the major part of my clay body. Naturally occurring stoneware clays are usually plastic, relatively strong, and fall within a reasonable cost range. Plasticity has always been increased, I've found, by lengthy soaking periods for freshly mixed clay, the addition of vinegar to the mix, and a great deal of spiral kneading. My practice has been to wedge and knead the clay after removal from plaster drying tables and to store it in large (10–20 lb.) balls, wrapped in moldy, damp towels, inside a large plastic bag inside a large cheese can or garbage can. Storing once-kneaded clay seems to improve the plasticity. When I need the clay for throwing, I knead it again and then ready it for the wheel by making the characteristic cannonball-shaped lumps. It sounds like a lot of energy being given over to clay preparation. It is. A good stoneware clay can be used after this kind of preparation with no additions. Since I usually add a red clay for color purposes when I fire with electricity, I also add fireclay to the clay body. The fireclay addition raises the temperature level of the clay body's maturation to a higher range (it is a very refractory type of clay), opens up the clay body, and adds a pleasant, rough quality (often described as toothiness) to the overall mix. The fireclay addition counteracts the tendency of the iron-bearing red clay toward lower maturation and toward surface slick. The rough-particled fireclay adds both strength in firing and textural quality.

You can achieve better clay bodies by knowing the traits of each clay in your mix. Awareness of individual clays' traits helps you to arrive at the clay that really suits your own sensibilities. Try to avoid complicating your clay by starting too abstractly: using ball clay for its plasticity, kaolin for strength or whiteness, then adding a red clay only for color, and then fireclay for tooth, and flint for increased silica. Staying close to a naturally occurring clay keeps your recipes and mixing operations in the realm of simplicity, cheapness, and comprehensibility. And if there is no reliable basic clay to start with? Your options are to get into more complex mixing operations or to buy prepared clay.

If you have no access to heavy mixing equipment, save your bread and buy prepared clay by the ton or half-ton.

Often a local supplier is willing to mix any clay body you like, if you promise to buy a large quantity. In any event, whether he prepares a body according to your own formula, or sells you one in his standard stock, it will cost you (at this writing) somewhere around ten cents a pound. A ton of clay will cost in the neighborhood of two hundred dollars. This may sound ridiculous both in quantity and in price, but that is a rough figure for what it will cost you if that is your only option. You are also paying for water, about 20 percent of the total weight in prepared clay. The clay comes in fifty-pound covered cans. Today, there is usually a large plastic bag around the clay inside the can. It keeps the clay fresh and moist for a long time. Open a few cans and disregard what your seller has told you. He will usually say that the clay doesn't need wedging or any other preparation before use. He's wrong. A lot of commercially prepared clay is mixed rather nonchalantly. It has a great deal of air mixed in and needs extensive kneading to make it truly plastic and wheel-ready. Knead the clay, divide it into large balls, wrap with a nice, moldy towel, put it all back in its bag, and close the can. Let it sit for a while, like a week or two. This seems to improve prepared clays to the point of true usability.

If you keep in mind the rough figure of $200 per ton for prepared clay, and add to it the fact that you're paying for water and maybe grog too, you'll probably be knocked over to learn that you can buy a ton of dry clay for about $75 to $80, or much less if you can get some people together and buy it by the carload (about 2½ tons). Of course, you have to mix the stuff somehow, supply the labor, water, grog, and cart it around. On the whole, though, it still comes out much cheaper to buy clay dry and mix your own, even with today's heavy freight costs. In the long run, experimenting and mixing your own clay produces a better clay than what is sold prepared.

If you are ready to produce in some quantity and have the bread there are clay-mixing machines. Paul Soldner is selling one (*Whole Earth Catalog*), bread-dough mixers are suitable, and then there are pug mills. New pug mills are extremely expensive. Bread-dough mixers are cheaper and you can still come up with one by haunting auctions. A friend of mine actually salvaged a pug mill from a local junkyard. If you are not as lucky, look around for an old-style, used, agitator-type washing machine. You can mix 40 to 50 pounds at a swirl with one of these things, and I've done 400 pounds by myself in a long morning. Washing machines yield a wet mix, but a denser mix than the plastic trash barrel-soaking method. A washing machine will not do what a mill or dough-mixer can do, but it works. You can get a month's supply of throwing clay with a hard day's work. The proportion of water needed will vary with different clay bodies, so my only recommendation is to remember to put water in first, about half a tubful. I usually add half a cup of vinegar to each tubful of water, before adding the dry clay. Gently add your clay mix in batches of about 10 pounds. When you've added about 40 to 50 pounds of dry clay, turn on the machine and let it get agitated. It needs only a few minutes to bat the sluggish mixture around. Clean out the clay and store it in your old, plastic trash barrel. Put some more water in the tub of the machine and gradually add your second 40 or 50 pounds of dry clay. Bat that around too. Empty the tub after a few minutes' mixing. You should have your large storage barrel in a convenient receiving position. You won't be able to move the barrel after it has 200 pounds of wet clay in it, so think beforehand about its position. You can fill a couple of barrels in three or four hours. You will see that this method moves faster, produces more mixed clay, and yields a less wet clay mix than the plain barrel-soak method. The clay will still be much wetter than clay coming from a dough-mixer or a pug mill. Excess water will rise to the top of the storage barrel in a few days. You can lay this clay out after five to seven days. It dries out to workability much faster than clay mixed by barrel-soaking. It may also have a lot more air in it from the agitated paddling. So it needs careful kneading.

Brickyards are hidden resources. Defunct yards are perfect for people who have no bread but must pot. In upper New York State there are a lot of old yards and some of them have adjacent clay banks, not in use. Ask for permission to dig the clay, it's usually up for grabs. Mixed by hand methods (barrel, etc.), with some fireclay and grog, these low-fire clays can yield usable mixtures. Test to ascertain the temperature range of your mix. I've used local red surface clays mixed with 20 percent of a fine grog up in the cone 4 to cone 5 range. If economy is your basic problem, try this as an option. As with digging clay directly from the ground, don't count on this alternative for strict uniformity of fired results.

USING THE CLAY

By now you have three or four hundred pounds of usable clay on hand. Wedge, knead, and age the clay to the best of your ability. You do not need a potter's wheel to use all your well-prepared clay. There are a few basic handbuilding techniques that require no wheel at all: primitive molds, pinch-potting, slab-building, coiling, and all combinations of the above. Starting backwards from the usual order in clay primers, I'll talk about simple molds. I do not mean to get into molds supplied by your local hobby dealer for slip casting, or the creation of plaster molds, on your own, for slip casting. When I talk of simple molds, I really mean simple. The simplest mold you can use is an old, worn-out, surface-eroded, wooden salad bowl. Spread a cotton rag out flat on a table. Take a two- or three-pound ball of wedged and kneaded clay, and either press it out flat on the rag (as with a bread dough) or roll it out flat on the rag by using a rolling pin. When you have a nice, even, ¼″ thick, overgrown pancake of clay, 5″ to 6″ wide, pick up the whole piece by holding on to the edges of the rag the clay was rolled out on.

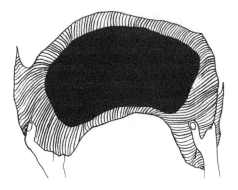

Place the whole thing, clay, rag and all, into the old salad bowl. Press the clay into the depths of the bowl and evenly out toward the side walls. Trim the excess clay from the top edge of the bowl. Let the rag hang out. It should look something like this:

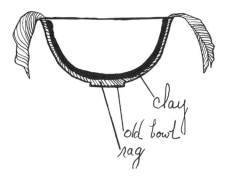

clay
old bowl
rag

Wrap the works up in plastic and don't look at it for a day. Come back to it the next day. Gently lift, by picking up the whole thing by the rag edges. If the clay has stiffened to the point where it lifts out of the wooden bowl easily and holds its shape, standing independently, gently pull away the ragging. Paddle the base of the released clay bowl until it is flattened out enough for the bowl to stand on securely:

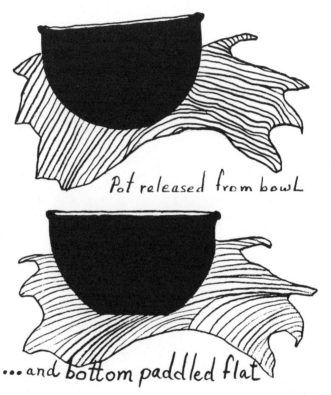

Pot released from bowl

...and bottom paddled flat

Such a molded bowl may be decorated by carving designs into the center or on the outside walls. It may serve as the base for a large pot. It is easy to add onto such a basic shape.

A simple plaster mold may be made by pouring plaster of Paris into a dish or plate lined with aluminum foil. When the plaster has set, the plate may be lifted away from the foil. Peel the foil from the plaster. Carve designs into the plaster (when damp). When the mold has really dried out (wait a day or two), roll out a slab of clay on a porous surface, to an even ¼" thickness. Let the slab stiffen somewhat and then lift it and press it against the plaster mold you've made. Press it evenly and firmly, all around.

Plaster Hump

.... Released, stiffened, new pot.

Paddle bottom flat or leave round (planter).

When the clay has stiffened to the leatherhard state, or a little harder (if you're not planning to do anything further to the piece), lift it off the mold. Trim and finish your piece.

These two mold techniques are ancient, simple, deal with plastic clay more directly than slip casting techniques, and are infinitely expandable and capable of variation. These kinds of molds yield all kinds of pots and unlimited creative potential. You can set them up in your kitchen or back closet if that's the only space you've got.

If you can envision your retired salad bowls, ashtrays, cracked soup plates, etc., coming back in new and splendid variations, you will have the basis of many, many pots to come. Handling the thin slabs of clay will teach you a lot about the strengths, capacity, and limitations of your particular clay, as you go on making pots. You can form the bases of many pots with these kinds of molds and then build up the walls with coils, thin leaflike slabs, or add on whole pinched-out pots.

These two mold techniques—the drape mold and the press mold—rely upon slabs of clay. Slabs of rolled-out clay may also be used independently of mold supports. Rectangular pots and square-shaped vessels may be hand-built out of slabs. Be sure to make very secure joins: score all edges and receiving points, add slip to the join if necessary, and roll shoestring-thin coils of clay to press into the corners when joining large slabs together. When rolling out the slabs, aim for evenness. Roll from the center outwards, toward the edges. Use guide sticks:

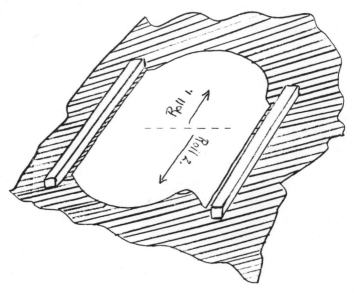

Aim for a thickness of approximately ½″. The walls of a piece built entirely of slabs, independent of any kind of support, have to be relatively thick. Use lots of grog. Grog will help the problem of dealing with thick walls when it comes to drying and firing slab-built pieces. It also helps to roll out slabs on a surface sprinkled with grog. The clay comes away from the surface very easily in that way. If possible, roll clay slabs out on porous surfaces, for easy lifting and the drying of excess water. But the right surface is not always at hand. Roll out slabs on textured cloths, such as burlap. This results in textural variety and helps the slabs stiffen. The fabrics absorb extra moisture from the clay. For easier maneuvering you can if you wish pick up the whole slab and fabric backing. If you fire with fuel you can incorporate the cloth in your pot; it will fire out. If you fire with electricity, use fabric Fiberglas in slab-building. It is a ceramic fiber product that adds support to slab-building and texture. It doesn't burn out, it begins to unite chemically with your work.

In general with slabs, use clay that is stiffer than you would use in throwing, coiling, or pinch-potting. Be patient with your clay when slab-building. Give it a chance to stiffen into the shapes you've created, before trying to add on, carve, paddle, or build up. When you've been working with thick slabs for a while, try using very thin little slabs and small units.

Coiling is a fundamental pot-making technique and a really basic learning experience in clay. It's the essential approach in any society that doesn't use the potter's wheel. The Indians of the Americas, tribespeople of Africa, and all the ancient cultures of the world made coil pots, and many still are creating coil vessels. Monumental pots and sculptures can be created with coils.

Coiling a pot consists of rolling out long snakes of clay (coils) and attaching them, one after another, to form the walls of a pot or other clay structure.

Scoring is basic to coil building: scratching deep lines on
a surface so as to make deep surface cuts. To make a se-

cure join between one coil and the next, score the top of the first coil with a slightly dampened toothbrush, thus making a network of scratched lines and moistened clay (slip). The slip acts as a glue, and the next coil, pressed firmly and deeply into the scratched lines, attaches securely to the lower coil. Try not to wet the clay too much when scoring and joining. If your coils seem to crack a lot on the surface, your clay may be too dry. Don't add a lot of water, it weakens the structure. Redampen all your clay before trying to go on.

Coils may be used for your entire vessel. Start a coil pot by rolling out a piece of clay for the base to a smooth, even thickness of ½″ to ¼″. Cut from this small, rolled-out slab the shape you need for the base of your intended pot, as though it were cookie dough. Place the base you've cut on a piece of unfinished wood or a plaster bat. Begin building the walls by rolling out coils and attaching them with the toothbrush scoring described above. If you want symmetry, rotate the wood or plaster bat your project rests on, as you build up with the coils. Very close symmetry may be achieved by using a template (a silhouette of your intended pot's profile). The coils may be anywhere from ¼″ thick to 1″ thick for very large-scaled pieces. Building with shoestring thin coils on a large scale is also possible: it moves slowly. The rhythms of the patterns of coils may be left as is, and utilized as a design feature and textural addition, or the coils may be smoothed down completely, inside and outside the pot, and the joins made completely invisible. I've found it helpful, from the structural point of view, to smooth the inside walls of coil vessels, even when intending to leave the coils visible on the outside.

Try experimenting with coils. Build with opened-up areas.

Press coils into other shapes such as cardboard boxes, fruit-crates, or old shards or bowls. When you set out to

coil your next pot, enlarge the scale of your accustomed work; double the width of your coils. See what the change of scale suggests. The next time around, divide ordinary coils into thin shoestring coils and create a pot with these. The strong contrast between very thin units and very thick coils will tell you a lot about weight, stress, and pace in coil-building. It also tells you a lot about ways to combine different techniques with coils as a bridge between, for example, thin-walled slab sections and a mold-built base with further coil-walled add-ons.

An entire pot may be "pinched" out of one single ball of clay. Start this one off with a prepared, wedged and kneaded, one-pound ball of clay. Wet your thumb slightly and then use it to burrow down into the center of the ball. Stop digging down when you feel you've come near the bottom, anywhere from ½" to ¼" from the bottom. Cradling the ball in one hand, move your other thumb out toward the sides of the ball, dragging clay across the bottom with it. Push the clay upward and outward, supporting this movement on the outside of the ball with your index and third fingers. Don't let the sides get too thin. Just keep moving the clay gently up and out. Rotate the ball as you push clay from the center out toward the walls with your thumb. You will soon have a shallow, hollowed-out bowl. Keep pinching until the walls are about ¼" thick all around. Set it aside for firming and a final shaping later. Try another pinch-pot. Only, the second time around, do it with your eyes closed. See if you can pinch out a small, even bowl, using no water, with your eyes closed. This trip will tell you a lot about the plasticity of your clay and the dexterity of your fingers. Pinching out a well-rounded tea bowl requires a lot of practice. Very large pots and sculptures may be created by pinching. Build up slowly toward larger projects by practicing many small ones.

And then there is pot-beating. Take a two- or three-pound ball of your prepared clay and beat it square, either by hitting it with a twine-wrapped paddle or club or throwing it down hard half a dozen times on your wedging table. When you've got a squarish shape that has a nice, distressed, banged-up looking surface, start carving it out. A melon ball scoop makes a good tool for a small pot. Hollow it out until the walls are between ½" and ¼" thick. Pierce the bottom in several places and you have a good planter for potting up cacti. Large sculptural pieces may be created this way, after some preliminary projects. And it lets out a lot of negative feeling, should the need arise.

Once you've made five or ten projects with each of the handbuilding methods described above, start combining techniques. A relaxed pace is the entire secret in handbuilding. Don't add onto a pot that is not firm enough to take additional weight. Let some more of its water escape. Keep several things going at the same time. As one firms up, work on another. And like a careful cook, keep a watchful eye on the condition of your works in progress. Try not to let large-scale handbuilt pots dry out too rapidly, or too much, if you're planning to increase their size, add handles, outgrowths, etc., decorate or carve. By experimenting with all these approaches you will really begin an intimacy with clay. It is this kind of ongoing tactile experience that will increase your understanding of clay. Compare your own first coiled or pinched pots with your pots of a year later. There it is.

III

Workshop Sites

ZONES

Country work sites do not pose the same kinds of problems as city sites. Zoning regulations don't impinge upon rural potteries in the same abundant and strangling degree that they impede the city potter. Cities often have tangles of overlapping prohibitions that require legal authorities for even minimal comprehension of the requirements. The greatest zoning hassles are natural-fuel fired kilns in cities. Then come problems of residential versus commercial zoning. These problems will vary in intensity and complexity with the degree of interest shown by your neighbors in your operations. If your neighbors dig having a potter next door, they probably won't hassle you about "light manufacturing" or selling from a residentially zoned location. Your landlord may not be as obliging. Don't sink any money into a location if you have doubts about it on this score. Think about zoning problems before you settle on your workshop site.

Zoning against natural-fuel kilns and foundries stems from days long gone but still has some validity from a safety standpoint, authorities in towns feel. Such installations were permitted only in areas zoned for industry or commerce, that had an assumed light residential density.

I would consider too today the fact that such kilns burn
something and thus add to the air pollution. When you
use an electric kiln there is pollution generated too, else-
where, where your power company burns fuel to generate
power. On the whole, I wouldn't get uptight about individual potters making smoke. Their contribution is minimal when you think of what one belch from your local
power company's smokestack sends into the air. But anything feels like a pollution addition in a city these days.
There's no greenbelt to utilize the potter's carbon dioxide
contribution. As far as zoning goes, electric kilns are nearly
universally acceptable.

DECIDING FACTORS

The major site factor to consider for setting up a pottery
that is going to depend upon electric kilns is the amount
and availability of power. Often in cities, apartments and
other multiple dwelling units do not have the capacity to
handle kiln operations. The wiring is rarely adequate. It
is not easy to obtain a landlord's consent to rewire your
own apartment for the kiln's demands. Often, landlords
are reluctant about permitting rewiring for kilns in apartments out of fear of fire insurance costs going up. They
are also uptight about any studio or commercial activity
going on in dwellings unless the dwellings fall into the
"professional" or "semi-professional" categories.

There are small kilns you can run on a 110–115 volt
standard apartment line, but your overall household wiring must be able to accommodate the heavy draw of the
kiln and the other household appliances simultaneously
(refrigerator, lights, etc.). These kilns are very small (usually no larger than 11″ x 11″) and will only go to the lower
firing temperatures. There are potters who work at home
but who do not fire or glaze their work at home. They

take their pieces to an outside facility for firing. Breakage in the transportation of ware is the main obstacle in such arrangements. If you have an apartment in a very old building and you wish to set up there, be very cautious about the wiring situation and make sure there is plenty of space between your intended kiln and the walls—18" or more.

There are definite advantages to setting up a workshop in your living place. Clay goes through so many changes and waiting periods that some potters find it works out well to have their studios where they live. They can be there at all the times their pots need looking after or checking out.

However, keep in mind certain physical problems involved in such an arrangement. The power factor added to the kind of pervasive dust-mess clay can make in a small dwelling often precludes setting up in the kitchen of your home. Clay dusts are a heavy thing to live with constantly.* The same is true of the ventilation problems presented by having a kiln of any kind going in your apartment or living loft. You have to make provisions for good ventilation during firings. If you use toxics such as white lead or potassium bichromate in your glazing, you have to be additionally cautious about ventilation, storage and cleaning procedures. If you have children and you

---

* Silicosis is a potter's occupational hazard, particularly for people working in cramped and ill-ventilated shops that are located in cities where there are substantial amounts of other pollutants in the air at all times. Technically, it is a disease of the lungs caused by the *constant* inhalation of dusts that contain a large proportion of inorganic matter (silica, asbestos, etc.). Environmental precautions are described as the best treatment—prevention is easier than cure. That translates into good ventilation, masks when mixing clay or glazes in great quantity, and a decided separation from your living (eating and sleeping) quarters. The dusts eventually drove my potting operations out of my kitchen-dining area into a rented workshop space.

plan to set up at home, it may be wisest to stay away from toxic compounds in your glazes altogether.

If you have some money and an interested friend or two, look for a commercial or industrial site. Try for a ground-floor location in a non-residentially zoned neighborhood. Look for good ventilation, solid flooring, hot and cold running water. These are essentials. Lighting, heating, and power are important too. Of course, try to rent as much floorspace as you can afford. The edges of cities are good places to check out when you start hunting for a pottery site. Defunct garages, light-manufacturing lofts, old storefronts, all make appropriate workshop sites and often have heavy-duty wiring, some ventilating apparatus, and the capacity to accommodate heavy floor loads. Locations on the fringes of a city or town are easily accessible to trucking.

Try to rewire if you can afford it. A new 110–115 volt circuit to accommodate power wheels, fans, a grinding wheel, and occasional usage of power tools, and a heavy-duty 220–230 volt line specifically for your kiln, will usually cover all your needs. Run your lights and small appliances on the house lines you find on the site. If and when you rewire, keep the bill down by situating your kiln as near to the meter and electric service basement of your building as possible (an advantage of ground-floor sites). You don't want to have to run expensive cables 25 or 50 feet more than necessary, or so far back as to require a transformer. If you find a workshop possibility with existing 220 volt lines, you're financially ahead.

If you find a site with all the other features—ventilation, water, good floors, spacious, light, and it's cheap—rent. It will be worth your while, over a long-run period, to pay for the wiring installation yourself. Landlords of commercial properties hardly ever object to your increasing the

value and safety of their properties by your installation
of new, competently done, more than adequate wiring.

Buy a good-sized, used fan and mount it in a transom
or window. When firing, use it on exhaust to draw out the
hot gases emitted by the kiln. An air-conditioning unit
would serve the same purpose if you have access to one
and the wiring to carry it. Generally, city potteries need
all the air openings possible. When you mix clays and
compound glazes, fine dusts fill the air. When you fire,
both heat and gases are emitted in quantity. And it's always good for you and the pots to see some sky and sun.
A natural-fuel kiln requires another kind of opening to
the outer world. A flue or chimney exit is needed for the
gases escaping from the hot kiln. So if you have any choice
available after considerations of power, floorspace and
water are resolved, pick the site with the most windows,
doors, skylights, old flues, etc.

Running water, both hot and cold, is basic. Many people
do without it in their studios. If, however, you plan to
produce in any quantity, you must have it, particularly
for glazing operations. You can make do with a rough cold
water hose arrangement or with carrying buckets for clay
mixing or even for throwing. When it becomes a matter
of glazing for two kiln loads a week you need running
water and warm water for clean-up operations. Try to
build your glazing table and glaze chemical supply shelves
near the sink to begin with; so that you save thousands of
steps in the end. A deep sink is a find. You can always buy
a substitute secondhand sink, if yours proves completely
inadequate. If you're thinking of such a change, call to
mind the high costs of plumber's services, before you decide.

On plumbing costs in general, don't have emergencies.
The way to avoid plumbing crises in potteries is not to

wash clay-covered tools, bowls, old glazes, or throwing-slop directly into the sink. If you wash clay and related materials down your sink constantly, and there is no trap provided, the clays will clog up your piping. This creates plumbing crises. If your sink has no trap you can empty out regularly, wash clayey things into a basin of water. Keep this basin in the sink or right nearby. Wash things in the basin and then under running water. The preliminary washing takes care of most of the clay and the residues settle to the bottom of the basin, not in your pipes. You can even reclaim the accumulated residues from the preliminary washbasin. Dump the sediments accumulated in the basin into your barrels of reconditioning clay. The minuscule amount of flux added to the reconditioned clay in the form of dumped glaze residues will not be enough to do anything radical to your clay body.

In some localities you will have to pay for your water. Check on this with your landlord, if and when you're renting a commercial property. Ask about the water-metering setup and rates, so that water costs don't come up as some sort of expensive surprise at some later date. For an individual studio setup you'll probably find that landlords absorb the costs (and simply pass it on in the rent). Another hidden small cost is the special tax some cities levy on commercial rental properties. Such taxes are usually a small percentage (1–2%) of yearly rental fees and are paid by the tenant to the city. Check this out before you get into it with a friendly lawyer or accountant.

Try not to build anything in if you are setting up a pottery on a short-term lease or nebulous friendly arrangement. Such items as plaster drying tables, work surfaces, damp boxes, and even kick wheels, may be designed and built so as to be movable, should it become necessary. These things are your fundamental work equipment, along with your kiln and possible mixing machine.

Every pottery needs some kind of plaster-surfaced drying table. This may be a small, portable slab of plaster
about 3″ thick, cast by pouring the plaster into a cardboard
box, or a table-sized slab. Such a surface is needed for
drying out clay, wedging and kneading. Decide about the
size of your plaster table by considering: your clay mixing
method; the kinds, scale, and number of pots you produce;
your overall available studio space.

You can cast and construct your own plaster drying
table by following the steps I'm outlining below. Adapt
the outline to your own needs. Build or select a form. I use
two-by-fours and plan upon a 3″ depth of plaster. I now
incorporate my casting form as part of the eventual permanent table structure. It is built of wood and braced on
the outside, if it is more than 18″ x 24″. Staple or tack
a layer of chicken wire or hardware cloth mesh to the
inside of the form. This reinforcement layer should be
tacked in at about the middle of the height of the form.
Place a piece of masonite or underlayment on a *level*
(really essential), surface. Grease the masonite with a
coating of paraffin or vaseline (I prefer paraffin). Place
the form upside down on the masonite; that is, with the
eventual top surface of the form face down. The masonite
should stick out from the bottom of the form on all sides,
by at least 2″ all around. Tack and caulk the form in place,
all around.

Get your interested friends together, water, 50 to 200
pounds of plain plaster of Paris (the amount depends
upon the size of the table you're planning). Do not mix
the plaster according to the package directions. Working
with a ratio of 8 ounces of water to every 1 pound of
plaster, compute roughly how much of each will be required to fill your form. Pour the amount of water you
need directly into your form. Add about a half cup of
vinegar to the water; this will retard the setting of the

plaster and allow you to maneuver out unevennesses. If all those gallons of water begin to seep a bit, tighten up the caulking job around the base of the form. Now, start sifting in your plaster. Go very slowly. At least three or four people, sifting together gently at separate points around the form, works best for large tables. When the water can no longer absorb any more dry plaster, stop sifting. Gently jiggle the whole works by moving the masonite base back and forth. Jiggling the whole form will help even out the pouring and let out trapped air.

Let it dry out for a few weeks, before touching it. Then upend the whole construction, untack, uncaulk, and pull back the masonite from the top. The surface should be level, hard and uniformly dense.

British potters tend not to use absorbent plaster surfaces as wedging surfaces, but many American potters use plaster for their wedging tables. I do use a plaster table for wedging; primarily because my clay mixing methods yield a relatively wet mix and the wedging-kneading process on plaster helps dry out the clay to a more workable throwing consistency. You can build and cast your wedging table in the same way as the drying table described above, or use part of your drying table for clay preparation. If you plan to do this, make sure you've reinforced the plaster with a good layer of wire mesh as described above. Your wedging surface will last much longer with a layer of mesh reinforcement inside.

Work tables are especially necessary when you do a great deal of handbuilding. I like to have one table that has a tough nonporous surface (such as enameled metal or formica), and a table that is relatively porous-topped. Unfinished plywood has been the cheapest, most durable, most useful porous surface I've used. It is more convenient to glaze on a nonporous surface: clean-up is faster and simpler. Coiling and general handbuilding are easier on wood surfaces. If you can manage it, try to have both available. If you do a lot of slab-building, you should consider bracing one of your tables into or against a wall. When you roll out slabs a lot, a stable table is a definite help.

The damp closet is discussed in the storage chapter and wheels in "At the Wheel."

Natural light is not as absolutely necessary to the potter as it is to painters. It is more a head need than a workshop necessity. Most ceramic decoration, "painting," and glazing is done with powdery suspension of glaze chemicals in water. The wet glaze mixtures you work with bear little resemblance to their eventual glassified forms and colors. You don't need steady, natural light when mixing or glazing. Good artificial light will suffice. You need good, steady illumination when throwing or building pots. I prefer daylight for these activities but it's hard to come by in ground-floor city potteries.

You are not absolutely bound to ground-floor sites. I've listed a lot of economic reasons for selecting ground-floor studios, but if the cost factor isn't too negative and you can find a place with an elevator (to move heavy bags of clay), a higher floor can work out. Do consider the prospect of getting quantity supplies to your studio. At first this may not be a problem because you're not doing quantity buying. The time will come, though, when you're into tons of clay. Truckers are not legally obliged to carry anything beyond the sidewalk of their destination addresses. Often, drivers do oblige you. But you can't count on it always. And what do you do with two tons of dry clay in front of your building when it is beginning to rain?

Think ahead to winter, if there is one where you live. Workshops should have some kind of heat. Don't depend on firing your kiln to heat your workspace. On the day when the kiln is cooling or no firing is going on, it will be cold. You don't need central heating since you're probably not in the workspace twenty-four hours a day. Think about it and work your thoughts into your budget and floorspace planning. If heat is provided by your landlord (it's in your rent costs), this isn't a problem. If not, consider a downdraft wood burner, if you have a flue, or small space heaters. My heating costs didn't come to more than a hundred dollars a winter for a 12′ x 55′ space with lots of leaks. It was heated 12 to 16 hours a day, and with old, inefficient gas radiators. So don't be put off if your prospective workshop has no steam heat supplied.

Finally, try to set aside a corner just to sit in—or a bench, or empty floorspace. I think it helps the work to have a place for sitting still somewhere in the workshop.

IV

Storehouse Thinking

FRESHLY MADE POTS

Potting requires as much accessory space as you can get. The work area, where you actually form and decorate pots, takes up less space than storing the pots while they go through all their necessary changes. The changes are promoted by there being enough room for all the pieces to do their shrinking, quietly and uncongestedly. Slow, even drying is helped along by flexible shelving arrangements and lots of shelf space given over to greenware. We built units that had ladder supports. The units accommodated movable shelves (from 24″ to 36″ long), usually two 8″ boards per level. Shelving should be made out of ¾″ exterior plywood, if you can get it. If shelves warp, pots stored on them to dry will warp. We scavenged all the plywood.

Movable shelves of this kind also make perfect boards to receive ware, when you're throwing lots of similar small things such as mugs or tea bowls. Set the boards down across the front of your wheel, throw, cut off, fill a board and return it to the wall unit, and take out the next one. Several levels of pots can be made, stored, and left to dry out evenly, within a short space of time. All the pots stored close together give off their water slowly and together. Usually they are ready for turning or handling

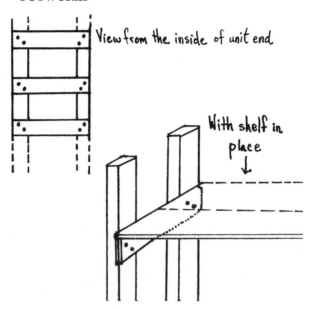

View from the inside of unit end

With shelf in place
↓

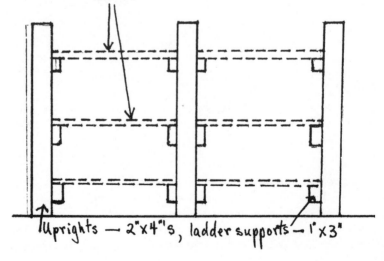

Rough of a unit to contain movable shelves

Uprights — 2"x4"s, ladder supports — 1"x3"

the next morning, without plastic wraps (unless you've been firing a kiln inside your workshop).

Large pieces, perhaps in the 18″ to 24″. range, may be stored within the same flexible unit by simply removing a few levels of shelving and standing the free boards aside:

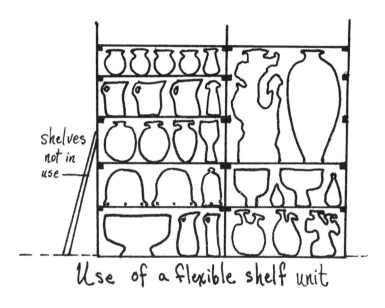

shelves
not in
use —

Use of a flexible shelf unit

Steel shelving units will serve some storage purposes but do not take the weight of damp clay perpetually. The shelves bend a lot and, of course, can't be moved in and out. Scale and amount of production determine how much shelving you will need. Flexibility is very important.

DAMP CLOSETS

Even if you're potting in a 12′ x 7′ closet-room, try to create a damp box of some sort for your pots in process. Such a storage box is necessary for slowly evolving pieces, handbuilt work, and lots of utilitarian wares like pitchers and teapots that need retarded, even drying of all their separate parts: lids, spouts, etc. I swear by damp closets. They provide protected, controlled drying and in that way prevent losses from cracking and the tensions produced by rapid drying.

Basically, a damp closet should have a poured plaster floor, shelves that can be moved in and out or put aside, and an accessible but easily protected location. If you have no niche available, build a pseudo-closet and use plastic sheeting stapled to two-by-fours for side walls.

If your kiln is inside your work area, a damp box is a necessity. Firing a kiln in tight quarters dries out the atmosphere so rapidly that work in process needs to be shielded or it will be lost. Plastic wraps and closeting-away have worked out best for me in that kind of situation.

Dampen the floor of your damp box frequently. This is done by soaking the plaster up to its absorption capacity. You want to keep the atmosphere in the closet happily humid. Movable shelves (if yours is that elaborate), preferably of exterior ply to avoid warpage, are best because they can double as ware-receiving boards when you are throwing. They are also good just because they're movable. You can take them out, stand them aside and dry out, slowly, a sculpture that is as large as the entire box. Pieces undergo fewer traumas if they are moved about on boards or bats, and not picked up and set down too often.

PLASTIC

Collect plastic sheeting, plastic laundry bags, huge dry cleaners' bags, kitchen wrappings, etc.; you'll need it all. Plastic wrap keeps clay and ware sufficiently damp to work at your own pace. If clay is allowed to dry out too fast, it will master your working schedules and processes for you. In centrally heated workshops, you can't simply let pieces dry out without protective measures. The drying happens too fast. This is a kind of seasonal and location problem. Just try to keep it in mind. Don't rush to blame all the cracks that appear in pots on your craftsmanship. Some of it has to do with work conditions. The natural rate of clay drying may work out well for you in a country, unheated, open situation, but it rarely does so in the city. So recycle some of the plastic and use it in your workshop.

After your pots are completed and ready to dry, invert them if the forms permit, and set them out on shelving to finish drying, as evenly spaced as possible. They should be bone-dry before bisque firing. Don't rush it. Inverting the ware evens out the drying process.

BISCUIT STORAGE

Storing once-fired pots is not as problematic or as space-consuming as storing unfired (green) pieces. Bisqued pots may be stacked one inside another and the storage shelves loaded densely. Once the pots are fired to bisque temperature they are not as fragile as greenware. However, once you've applied glazes to the bisqued pots they can't be piled one inside the next. The glazed bisque ware can't touch or the dry powdery glaze coatings will be rubbed off. Pots that have had their glazes applied and are waiting for a glaze kiln stacking and firing, again, take up a lot of shelf space, much more space than unglazed bisque.

This is a temporary problem, because these pots are on their way to a firing, but keep it in mind. If possible, set up a few movable shelves on bracketing close to the kiln. These shelves will accommodate glazed bisque wares before the firing, keep them out of the way of other operations and provide a convenient loading situation when you are stacking the glaze kiln.

FINISHED POTS

Storage of finished ware becomes a real problem in tight city spaces. If you don't have a small area for display purposes, try everything to move your finished pieces out: perpetual loans to friends, sales, fairs, consignment, gifts, attics, all come in handy. Once you are throwing proficiently and glazing competently, you will soon find that your finished work accumulates really fast. Don't let it push you out of your workspace. Try not to be precious about your pots. Keep what you like most and move the rest out.

STORING MATERIALS

After a time, I was buying clays and glaze materials in quantity, by the ton. I had a basement, 10′ x 16′, at my studio, in which I stored all the raw materials. It meant a lot of dragging of sacks up and down cellar stairs and excursions to fill smaller containers with chemicals every now and then, but the availability of storage space made it easy to buy ceramic materials dirt cheap. Nothing but water can harm dry materials; not cold, heat, nor wind. If you keep dry materials in a basement, put them up on platforms, four to six inches off the ground. Rain seeps down through cellar doors, water pipes break, and piping sweats. Keep all that damp in mind if you plan to utilize any kind of below-ground storage.

If your raw materials are stored in your workshop, they will take up room in the work area but will be readily accessible. Try keeping stacks of sacks under work tables and shelving.

If you buy glaze chemicals in quantity, you will need a series of small containers that you can keep on very accessible shelves in the workshop. I use gallon jars that I get from local luncheonettes and restaurants. Fill the gallon jars with frits, spars, kaolins, etc.—whatever you use frequently—and label them in some systematic fashion and set them on shelves in a place convenient to the sink and table used for glazing. Plastic gallon jars are more durable than glass, and safer, but glass is much easier to clean. Take what you can get. If only a few plastic gallon jars come your way, reserve them for storing wet, mixed glazes.

GLAZE STORAGE

I don't mix glazes in very large amounts because I am not a production potter. Two thousand grams of dry glaze materials and the requisite amount of water for proper consistency will fill a gallon jar comfortably. This tends to be my unit because of storage convenience. I dip most of my utilitarian pieces so I need more glaze on hand than a potter who relies on pouring for his major glaze application technique. Gallon jars of glaze work out well for my needs. I only use storage jars that can be tightly closed. Many potters use large stoneware crocks for glaze storage but I find the evaporation, settling, and hardening that occurs from loose cover fit a storage nuisance. They're a lot nicer to have around and look at than gallon mayonnaise jars. In any event, mix your glazes and glaze your pots. Whatever glaze is left over—save. Pour the remaining glaze back into the jar and screw the lid on tightly. It will keep for the next glazing session. Recondition your leftovers every few weeks, so as to avoid the settling out of heavy glaze ingredients, if your glaze firings are infrequent. Mixed glazes in their wet state can be stored away easily. Stack the tightly covered jars under tables, in cabinets, out of the way of the forming or throwing of new pots. The jars needn't take up much room but can still be easily available.

KILN FURNITURE

When you're through providing storage for all the things I've listed, think about putting your kiln shelves and supports in a good place. These items won't always be in the kiln. Find an out-of-the-way, protected location for them. Fit them into the storage scheme and they will never get lost or broken.

As you can see, there's lots of stuff accumulating around any potting activity. If you can get into providing spaces beforehand for all the pots, processes, materials, and stages, your working time will be free and happy.

V

Scavenging

Scavenging is a necessary and health-giving activity for the potter. In these times of affluent absurdity, the potter can do more than just an individual's share of pollution prevention. City potters do have an advantage over rural clay workers in this one respect. There is a thousand times more "waste" in a great city than there is in the country. There is also a large concentration of "junkyards" in and around larger cities. There is a constantly transient population moving about cities, throwing away hundreds of pounds of good and useful "trash." Often it is more costly to move or store big old things in a city than it is to buy new ones. So more people throw more things out.

All the words set off in quotes are being written that way to emphasize their definition as trash by some people and their definition as finds by others. Tons of useful "waste" are thrown out daily in cities. Potters, as persons who respect the environment, can recycle for their own use: glass jars (all sizes and types), plastic containers, coffee cans, old cooking pots, pans, barrels, basins, ladles, spoons, sticks, worn tools, discarded bearings and discarded hardware, kitchen wares (rusted sieves, measuring cups, spatulas), lengths of pipe, worn screening. All these things are useful in a pottery workshop. Raw glaze materials, pigments, mixed glazes, test batches, all need storage

71

containers. It is plain wasteful to spend any money for jars or other containers. Check out your local delicatessens and luncheonettes for emptied gallon jars. Usually, food places throw out once-used, perfectly good, mayonnaise or pickle jars at the end of every working, eating day. Take up collections among your friends. They'll be glad to get rid of all those jam, relish, sauce, and baby food jars that accumulate so fast. Coffee cans in their new plastic-topped form are really handy-sized containers for coloring oxide storage.

Basins, pots, pans, ladles, spoons, and scoops of any sort are needed for glaze mixing and application. Worn-out blades and tools, all sorts of hardware miscellany are useful in potteries on an erratic basis. They will not be heavily worked, just used here and there; for sawing an insulating brick into sections or other such small jobs. Pieces of used screening may be set into wood framing if you don't have the bread for an expensive lab quality sieve or brass sieve cloth. Lengths of piping are good for supports and as stirrers. Textural effects in clay can be achieved by pipe beatings.

So-called "used" wood is always available and immeasurably utile. Skids are crude, wooden platforms used wherever fork-lift loading goes on: near docks, near printing or paper concerns. These platforms make perfect supports for stacked 50- and 100-pound bags of dry clay. Often the clay storage site of a pottery has an uneven or damp floor. Skids used in this way keep your materials dry and available. Many people I know in New York City use them for heating fuel. Burning skids sends particulate matter into the air but gets them off the streets. Burning skids releases smoke but you can recycle the ash into glazes and gardens. If you need a large, heavy-duty, plaster drying and wedging surface, consider using a skid for your form. Reinforce it and pour the plaster directly into it.

Plywood sheeting is discarded regularly in New York City. Film and television studios throw out once-used plywood, masonite, and lengths of two-by-four, and other sound structural materials. These materials are used for sets for films and TV commercials. The sets are too cumbersome and expensive for space-starved N.Y.C. studios to store, so they pass the costs on to their customers and just throw the sets out after minimal use. You won't believe the excellent quality of these throw-aways until you get out there yourself and start scavenging. We've retrieved entire 4' x 8' sheets of ¾" exterior plywood (thrown out after two days' service—they were "used," i.e., painted on one side). All of these materials are important and useful in shop construction, which does seem to go on forever in potteries. Shelving, siding for damp closets, table tops, reinforcement and shimming, wooden forms for casting plaster, planks for chutes, all needs arise eventually.

Junkyards are treasure-troves. All the parts for your kick wheel, even bearings, can come from junk. Look for industrial flywheels, old cistern covers, tractor seats, shafts, pipe lengths. Beat-up brick and cement blocks are always good for supports or display props. Slate slabs from steps or old fireplace mantels are often found just for the moving. They require much work to clean (and some muriatic acid), but yield solid display shelves for heavy pots. If you have access to heavy equipment, such as an oxyacetylene outfit, there is no end to the metal material you can efficiently recycle for pottery purposes in your workshop.

The best source for weathered wood in the New York area is one of the world's greatest natural junkyards, South Beach on Staten Island. All the crap in New York Harbor makes its way there and some of it stays on to weather. Good display props and mounts for sculpture (as well as the stuff of sculpture itself) are abundant. The

wood is usually heavily textured and makes great imprint-
ing tools for slab pots and clay reliefs. Soak it in Clorox
or other fungicidal solution before use.

All old clothes are particularly useful; either as protective garments when you're working or slopping around
in the clay, or as rags. Collect old draperies, kitchen towels,
diapers. Heavily textured fabrics make good texturing surfaces, tacked onto boards, when you are rolling out slabs
of clay. I also use old, preferably moldy, rags to wrap clay
in during my clay's aging sessions. The various organisms
alive in the rags help the aging-plasticity processes go on
in your clay. Dampened rags placed inside slowly evolving
handbuilt clay pieces aid in evening out the drying rate
or keeping the work wet enough to be worked on over
very long periods of time. Ragging can also be used as
supportive stuffing for the insides of large hollow built
projects and can be drawn out like surgical packing, when
the piece is self-supporting. Large rags are also necessary
if you work with drape-molds to any degree. Old crocheted
doilies make networks of fine decorative imprints when
pressed into damp clay.

Paper bags should be salvaged. Collect them at home
and from your friends. Bring them to your workshop. For
the first two years of my selling career I was able to wrap
all my pots in newspaper and pack them in second-go-
around brown paper bags I had collected. Newspaper,
too, can serve as supportive armatures inside large pieces.
I also use old newspapers and large bags to cover stored
bisque when I need my plastic sheeting for projects still
in the wet stages. Cardboard boxes are useful for storage,
packing, and mailing pots. Try them as building forms too
for large garden-sized pots. Your local liquor store has
hundreds of waste cardboard boxes.

Overcome all scruple about secondhand things and
teach yourself to use everything that comes your way.

VI

At the Wheel

I've decided to write an involved wheel chapter for people who have been throwing for a while; who have discovered that they love the wheel, want to make quantities of pots, and therefore need dependable, steady access to wheels or their own wheel. Great pots have been made for centuries without using the potter's wheel. If you can't afford the one you want now, or have no place to put it, are not physically into it, hate machines, don't like symmetry, don't get a wheel at all. Put your energy or money into a good kiln.

My feeling, generally, is that power wheels are not for beginners. It isn't impossible to learn to throw on a motorized wheel. It just seems to be a harder way for many beginners. Electric wheels seem to "get away" from novices, are too fast, or too insensitive for many people new to throwing. In my experience, beginners' pots are definitely more squat and bottom heavy when thrown on a power wheel than are the pots made by novices on kick wheels.

KICK WHEELS

A kick wheel is a simple machine, powered by you. A basic, sit-down kick wheel consists of a flywheel, a wheel

75

head (on which the clay is worked), a shaft uniting these
two parts, bearings (to mitigate the friction generated by
the turning shaft), and a frame on which all the other
parts are hung. There are many types of kick wheel. The
type I find most enjoyable and efficient is one in which a
part of the frame supports a seat for the potter and part
of it holds up a table for the ware (and maybe a catchall
under the wheel head). The major function of the frame
structure however, is to support the spinning shaft in a
vertical position. Such a basic kick wheel looks like this,
viewed from the outside:

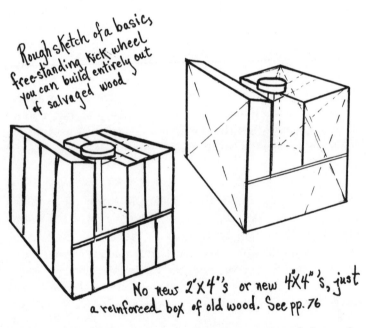

Rough sketch of a basic
free-standing kick wheel
you can build entirely out
of salvaged wood

No new 2"X4"'s or new 4"X4"'s, just
a reinforced box of old wood. See pp. 76

and like the drawing on the next page, viewed from the
point of view of its essential structure.

When planning a wheel, focus your design energies on
this essential shaft support structure. All the other frame
parts of the wheel are of secondary importance.

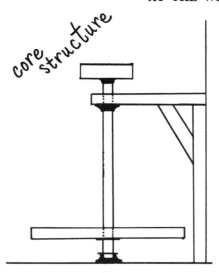

core structure

It is possible to construct a serviceable, efficient, durable, first wheel from junk. The junk must be carefully selected. I guess this raises it into the category of "scrap" rather than junk. The essentials you must gather together are: two good bearings, a shaft, a flywheel, a wheel head, scrap lumber, nails, screws, and nuts and bolts. Suggestions as to specific materials that fill the bill are given as I go on in this chapter. You will need some basic tools. At the barest minimum, you will need a hammer, a handsaw, a square, a plumb line, screwdriver, and a level; and perhaps a book to teach you how to use them if you've never used these tools before. A book I recommend is *How to Work with Tools and Wood* by Robert Campbell (a paperback cheapie). If you've done no building or woodworking before this, you should be aware that you are taking on an ambitious project. Small-scale power tools such as an electric drill and a power handsaw will help you build faster and expedite a number of alternatives, if you're working with salvaged materials. For example, the power tools make possible the use of found cement flywheels or steel and plywood combinations for flywheels:

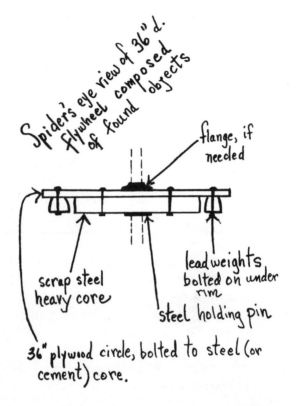

Spider's eye view of 36"d. flywheel composed of found objects

flange, if needed

scrap steel heavy core

lead weights bolted on under rim

steel holding pin

36" plywood circle, bolted to steel (or cement) core.

You can salvage all the parts needed. If you do choose to spend some money, put it into bearings; sealed, permanently lubricated, self-aligning bearings.

CONSTRUCTING A FIRST WHEEL

Consider where the wheel is to stand. The prime location for a wooden frame wheel is butting into a corner. That means there will be two walls available for supportive help. The support I look for is not standing support but the supportive ability of the walls to absorb the shocks of kicking. The constant strain of a full-time potter kicking can shake a wood frame structure apart. The optimum place for a wooden frame wheel is where there is a wall ahead of the wheel and a wall to the right of the wheel, if you throw and kick righthanded. The walls are your shock absorbers in this situation.

One wall straight ahead to butt the structure into will suffice, too. The more you utilize the existing structures (walls, floors) to support your wheel frame, the fewer structures you must supply. That means savings in lumber and energy and labor.

The least promising situation is the completely independent, free-standing, wooden structure. The best approach to the free-standing situation is to rely on steel pipe for the frame. Welded metal supportive structures are much more durable in a free-standing situation than are wood structures. The Soldner wheels are good examples of this type of wheel. However, home constructed welded metal wheels assume you have an oxyacetylene outfit or similar equipment. Not many people have access to a torch.

The best specific plan for a cheap, free-standing wheel of wood frame construction that I've seen is to be found in Jon Kaplan's 1970 article on building a wheel in issue number 6 of *Mother Earth News*, pp. 69–74. His design is functional and easy to construct. It assumes some prior building experience or the help of a more experienced person. I think his plans ought to be modified along the following lines:

a) increase his suggested flywheel diameter of 24″ to a diameter of 32″ to 36″

b) increase his suggested flywheel weight to 130–150 pounds

c) add the increased weight around the rim of the flywheel and distribute it evenly around the underside edge

d) the enlarged flywheel requires an overall increase in the lengths of the horizontal wood members; from his 30" cube construction to a 34"–38" length for the horizontals (depends on the eventual diameter of your flywheel selection)

e) the bracing could be improved, especially if you intend to give the wheel heavy, daily use.

The theory behind the recommended flywheel changes is that a wider, heavier wheel with a large part of the weight at the rim of the wheel has better velocity and momentum. You'll get more turning force for your kicking energy. Placing the mass of a flywheel as far as practicable from the center of rotation (such as in the rim) produces more power from your kick. Weight increase at the rim may be achieved by setting in a salvaged steel ring, lead weights, or any heavy scrap you weigh out and distribute evenly at the circumference when you cast the wheel. See flywheel diagram above.

The construction of Jon's wheel does depend on purchasing new bearings, a purchased shaft, and to some degree on new lumber and a new wheel head. If you scrounge all the lumber, you can build Jon's wheel or the one discussed below for the price of the bearings alone. I suggest, when using salvaged lumber, that you box the entire wheel in for reinforcement or sheathe it and use the cross-bracing sketched at the beginning of this chapter. You won't have to depend on the strength of newly purchased lumber but you can still utilize the *Mother Earth* plans.

Such a reinforced wood frame wheel will serve your needs, unless you envision six to ten hours of constant everyday use. You can also avoid elaborate reinforcement if you bolt your lower wheel bearing into the floor, rather than into the bottom of your wheel structure. I realize this isn't always feasible for people (rented spaces, cement floors, or fancy apartment parquet). However, if it is possible for you, some of the stresses of kicking can be minimized by securing the bottom bearing to the floor. In such an arrangement, the floor absorbs some shock and the wheel needn't be as heavily built and braced as a totally independent wheel. Again, this means savings in materials and labor. Plus, the advantage is in the lessened wear and tear on the frame structure; much less tightening and retightening of the nuts and bolts that usually hold free-standing wheels together.

The following wheel plans were designed for a specific location that utilizes a wall ahead of the wheel and the floor below. In addition to materials and labor savings, the design has the advantage of placing a rather large tool (36″ diameter flywheel) in an integrated architectural setting in the workshop. Even though it has a large flywheel, this wheel takes up less working space than most free-standing wheels. I've presented it here in a general way, so that a reader and builder can grasp the ideas and adjust the specifics in relation to the structures and workspace available in any projected studio. I've also included the nagging details of setting up the steps in building a wheel. Plans have been available, but details of the execution of the designs haven't been as available. My plan concentrates on the design and setting up of the essential structures of the potter's kick wheel: creating a support to hold the shaft vertical; the bearing, shaft, flywheel relationships; and some advice on bracing. There is also attention given to that always glossed-over hassle: how to get an inexpensive wheel head on an inexpensive wheel.

The structure that supports the shaft is a length of two-by-six that is placed far enough away from the wall to allow for easy clearance of the flywheel. For example, if your flywheel has diameter of 36″, and thus a radius of

18″, the supportive shaft arm will have a length of 18″ plus some clearance inches at the wall end, and 1½″ to 2″ where the arm crosses the vertical support; in the diagram the total arm length is R + A + C + B. It totals 24″ on my wheel. At the *A* end there should be room enough around the shaft hole to support the upper bearing.

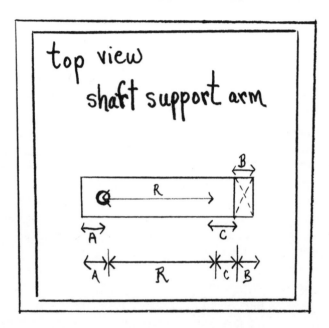

A hole is to be cut in this support arm, large enough for the shaft to pass through. It should be slightly larger than the diameter of the shaft you choose. If your chosen shaft has a diameter of 1″, the hole should be 1¼″. The hole must be cut out before you place the arm in position.

The bearings for this wheel are discarded VW throw-out bearings. You can salvage these from a local VW servicing place. They're no longer up to carrying a 2,000+ lb. vehicle on the road, but they are adequate for use

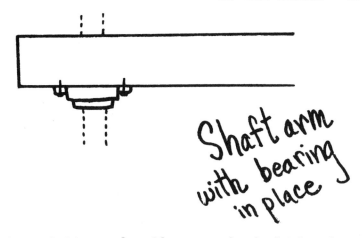

Shaft arm with bearing in place

in a primitive machine like a potter's wheel. These bearings are not set in flanges. They do have a helpful extrusion on each side. I attached them to the shaft arm and later to the floor by using ⅜" copper tubing staples on each side of the bearing.

Place one bearing in position on the underside of the shaft arm.

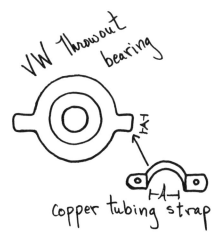

VW Throwout bearing

Copper tubing strap

The shaft arm is tied into the wall as in the diagram below. It is placed 34″ off the ground.

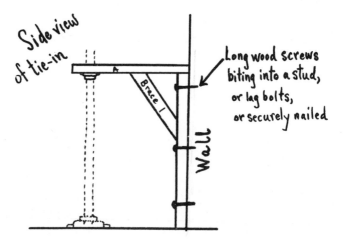

Please notice that your nails or screws bite into studs in the support wall. A clearer view of the tie-in and bracing is in the following top-view drawing:

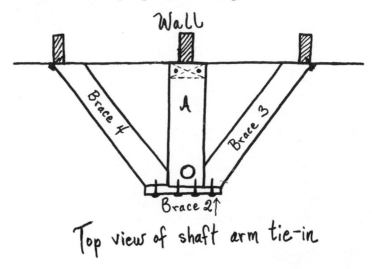

Test to see whether the shaft arm is securely tied in by grabbing it and trying to shake it from side to side. A little play is cool. Any real movement from side to side indicates that firmer bracing is needed.

Once the shaft arm is secured to the wall, the next step is to mark the position of the floor bearing. Placing the bottom bearing on the floor with the shaft in it, plumb the shaft with a carpenter's level. Mark the position of the floor bearing when you are sure the shaft is plumb. Withdraw the shaft and secure the bottom bearing by screwing down the copper holding staples. Put the shaft through again and make a final check. This alignment process is absolutely critical for any wheel utilizing bearings that are not of the self-aligning type. Even self-aligning bearings and their shaft should be aligned as precisely as you can get it initially. It is much more of a sweat working it out with salvaged bearings.

For the shaft of this wheel, I've utilized 1″ galvanized pipe. Its actual total outside diameter is 1⅝″, a factor that's given us hardware-fit hassles, but the shaft is a fair fit with the salvaged bearings. The bearings determine most of your choices in an enterprise that is based on scavenging. In my case, I still had a slight fit differential to compensate for; the shaft being slightly smaller than the bearing opening. A sheet of paper wrapped once around the shaft made up the difference, which tells you how slight the differential actually was.

The shaft is not to touch the floor. There would be too much friction for it to turn. Drill a hole through the shaft, through which a steel holding pin can be inserted. It keeps the shaft from hitting the floor (see p. 86).

The flywheel should be heavy. The weight should be equally distributed with some added weight emphasis around the rim, if you can manage it. I like a weight somewhere between 130 and 150 pounds and a diameter of

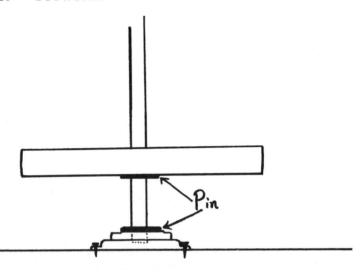

three feet. The specific weight and diameter are up to the individual potter, space considerations, and the materials salvaged. The flywheel can be cast cement; Sakrete with a layer of hardware cloth or wire mesh makes a good wheel. You should have the time and room to cure it, if you plan to cast a cement flywheel. There are fairly explicit casting instructions in Jon Kaplan's abovementioned plans. I would, as I have said before, plan to increase the flywheel weight and diameter. Plan to utilize up to 120 pounds of dry cement ready mix.

The flywheel I settled on for this project is sketched out early in this chapter. I discuss it in a more detailed way further on. I wish to continue by mentioning other materials you can scrounge for to utilize as a flywheel or the weight core of a flywheel.

Access to a welder's torch makes it feasible to use almost any heavy steel you can salvage. Before getting into a metal flywheel though, it is really best to make sure you have that torch or welder's skill available to you. There's lots of lugging and planning involved if you are going to employ steel scrap for this purpose. Outside fabrication or welding may be needed for this option, but sometimes the cost is minimal.

Precast cement cistern covers, old well covers, slate table tops are all viable possibilities. The cement covers can usually be handled by you if you have an electric drill with a masonry bit. You can drill out the shaft hole yourself. Utilizing slate rounds involves lots of determined, long-hour chipping to do a shaft hole. Junkyards often yield old flywheels from industrial machines. There are always flywheels to salvage from defunct potters' wheels. You'll find something appropriate once you start looking.

The flywheel for this wheel is an 85-pound steel manhole cover, bolted to a thirty-six-inch ¾" exterior grade plywood circle, with 40 pounds of lead weights bolted to the underside of the outer rim of the ply circle. I prefer kicking on wood surfaces to kicking on metal. Everything was scavenged. I paid eight dollars for steel fabrication, to have a shaft hole bored through and four bolt holes drilled in the manhole cover. This was the only cash expenditure in the entire project.

This flywheel is weighted more heavily at the rim with eight 5-pound lead weights bolted to the ply circle. Again, this places the greater weight farther from the center of rotation. These weights are spaced evenly out near the perimeter of the flywheel. You can melt scavenged lead or use plumber's pigs. The flywheel must have a hole for the shaft cut or cast into it. The fit must be as nearly perfect as possible to prevent wobble. The distance between the shaft arm and the flywheel is determined by the length of the potter's leg, i.e., your comfort (see p. 88).

The last step is to place the wheel head. If you are using galvanized pipe for a shaft, thread it at the top end. Or work with a pipe length that is already threaded at one end. The easiest way of attaching a wheel head to this

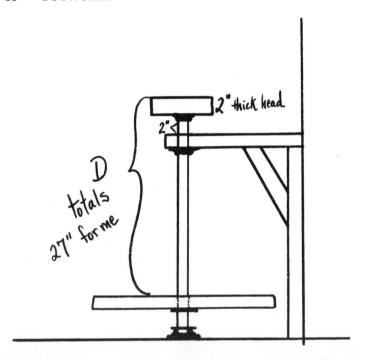

type of shaft is with an appropriately sized floor flange. The floor flange is screwed or bolted to the underside of the wheel head. The flange has to be centered accurately. The wheel head, with its floor flange underneath, is then screwed onto the threaded top of the shaft. A 2″ clearance between the head and the shaft arm is allowed.

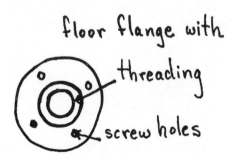

HEAD HASSLES

For this wheel I used a 2″ thick, 11″ diameter, solid circle of rock maple for the wheel head. It is the fanciest bit of scavenging ever achieved in this pottery. I have nothing against cast metal wheel heads except their current cost.

Maple, oak, or any other hardwood you can procure can be used as a wheel head and attached by the flange method I have described. A woodworking friend with a band saw or a large-scale lathe will expedite the turning of a hardwood wheel head.

If you cannot work out a wood head arrangement, I suggest casting an extra-dense plaster wheel head. This head goes back to the old wheel of a friend of mine, Pat Chandler Doran of the first Sixth Street Pottery.

The recipe for a dense plaster is mine, a modification of the nearly chip-proof bat-casting recipe I've evolved over the years. Some of the bats in my shop are eight or nine years old and unchipped. The casting method sounds weird and counter to anything you've ever read but that's how I cast all my bats and nearly indestructible wedging and drying tables.

Planning for a 2″ thick head with a diameter of 12″, prepare a mold of masonite and a 3″ band of linoleum.

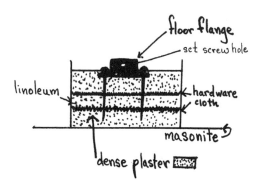

Coat the inside by rubbing it down with a block of paraffin. Staple in a layer of hardware cloth, 1½" below the top edge. Place the mold on a level surface. Fill it with a mixture of 56 ounces of water and 3 ounces of vinegar. Gently sift in 8 pounds of ordinary plaster of Paris. When all the plaster is sifted in, jiggle and wriggle the mold to encourage trapped air to surface. Place the flange on the surface of the plaster. Center it precisely. Press in till the flange section is almost completely covered and embedded in the plaster. Press in 2" wood screws through the flange holes, into the plaster. The vinegar is added to the water to retard the plaster setting so that you can place and anchor the flange. Now let it all set.

Tear the linoleum and masonite away after two days. Don't use the head for a few weeks. Then screw it onto the threaded top of the shaft. Plaster heads will not endure the way a metal or hardwood wheel head lasts. They are a cheap solution to the problem of finding a cheap wheel head. They're good to throw on because they absorb so well. And they're easily replaced when the necessity comes.

When using standard threaded flanges as a solution for attaching the wheel head I think it is advisable to provide against any tendency they may have toward unscrewing and loosening on the shaft. A hole should be tapped in the side of the flange to accept a standard set screw. Or a hole can be drilled through the flange and shaft and another of our steel holding pins inserted. Some of our shafts have many holding pins in them. They resolve many flywheel and head holding difficulties.

The total length of the shaft can be roughly three feet. This will allow for a lot of individual variation. Now, check to see if the wheel head is level. If the bearings and the shaft have been properly aligned, the wheel head cast on a level surface, the top of the wheel head should check out as level.

A seat and footrests are added:

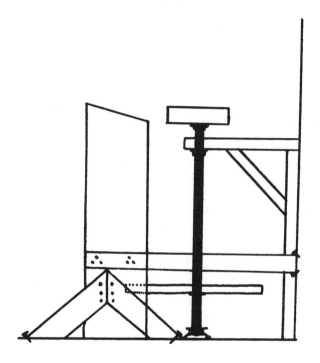

The seat should place you so that you can hang over the wheel head, easily and comfortably. Preferably it should place you so that you can bend fully from the waist, when necessary. Bending from the upper or midback for heavy jobs like centering big amounts of clay creates lots of backaches, especially for women. The seat has to be braced so that there's little or no movement. Cross-bracing at the rear and triangle braces at the base of the seat should be adequate. The footrest cross-pieces should, ideally, tie into the studding of the opposite wall.

If the above design doesn't suit you or your location, you can easily modify it. It was designed by a friend of mine, Lou Talento, and you have his permission to use it as is or work out changes from it.

Another simple modification, aside from changing the location, is to spend money for permanently lubricated, self-aligning bearings. You have to align them properly, initially. However, these bearings do make up for one's inability to construct the perfect precision alignment, for they adjust and compensate. So, if you are at the point where you wish to construct a lifetime wheel, spend for excellent bearings. A set of these cost me thirty dollars over eight years ago. With inflation, I'd imagine they're near forty or fifty today. Needless to say, the building advantage is that you can choose bearings with appropriate flanges for your design; rather than design around the bearings.

You can also purchase a solid steel shaft, and have it machined to your specifications, pin-holes drilled through, etc. If you are going this far, you can buy a whole wheel kit to assemble, too. I preferred building my own kick wheel initially and did it the first time for only the cost of the bearings. The wheel in this chapter was built to demonstrate that it is possible to recycle American junk into a useful tool and to explicitly delineate the process.

When I was sitting in my shop with two hundred dollars in hand after a particularly frenzied Christmas-time sale, I decided it was going toward the purchase of an electric wheel. It was a promise to myself; that I would not go into heavy production period again without an electric wheel.

THE MOTORIZED WHEEL

Basically, I'm prejudiced against electric wheels. My teachers inculcated me with the bias, but I have my own gripes against them. There is not much sensitivity in the down range on most electric wheels, even my current favorites. For turning, for throwing globes, delicate bottles, and thinner wares generally, I still use a kick wheel. For the quantities of mugs, bowls, jugs, planters, and other utilitarian pots that are the sales backbone of many potteries, I use a power wheel.

Motorized wheels are expensive. That's my other main gripe about them. It's not something that is much cheaper to build at home, either. Unless you have come into a good variable speed motor for little or no cost, an electric wheel you build yourself can run over $200. For $200 you can buy a high quality, little-used, dependable "brand" wheel, secondhand.

Power wheels that have any sensitivity of response, a smooth gradation of reactions as you pass from low to high speeds, solid construction and design, are going to be costly. Most good electric wheels list at about $350 and up, new. Add on shipping and taxes, those painful, hidden costs, and you're in the $400 range. By the time this book is published, inflation will probably have driven these stated prices up somewhat. If you are planning to buy a new wheel, you have to be considering at least a $400 expenditure. I'm not writing a brief for specific wheel manufacturers, but the truth is that not all the electric wheels on the market are worth the $400 or more that is asked. So I'm sticking my neck out and listing by brand name, and in the order of my personal current preference, wheels I recommend you investigate before buying:

Shimpo
Skutt
Alpine
Denver Fire Clay

Try all of these out before selecting one. If you're into the kick-motor combination type wheel, try out the Randall wheel too. I have my personal prejudices, strong likes and dislikes on the subject of power wheels. It's the price thing in the background that is always making me gulp and find fault, I'm sure. All I wish to do here is pass on to you my more positive experiences. Perhaps it will help someone before taking a big plunge. The wheel I prefer now, across the board, with few quibbles, is the Shimpo. The ring cone design makes for smooth gradation. It is a sturdily designed and executed wheel, highly portable (which is becoming important now that kilns can move too), and it still is up to taking a terrific amount of heavy production wear and tear.

It is usually possible to find a little-used, good quality, electric wheel secondhand. In New York City a couple of years back you could always find a relatively new Shimpo going secondhand. It's not a novice's wheel. So there was something of a market in mistakenly purchased Shimpos. It does take hunting and knowledgeability to find a good motorized wheel secondhand. Look for manufacturers you can rely on, take someone more expert with you, have a diverse experience of power wheels yourself, know your dealer.

Don't buy it without trying it, no matter how tempting. Bring some of your usual throwing clay along, wedged, kneaded, and balled-up, when you go to meet the wheel. Throw on it for a while, large pots and small. Listen for possible grating sounds when you change speeds. Watch out for wobbles, possible shaft distortions. Upend the wheel after the throwing session. Check out the fan belts or rubber discs. See whether the motor is reasonably clean-looking and the innards unencrusted. See whether you like the feel of the wheel. If you slip into an easy, comfortable, working relation with the wheel, it may be the one you need and will enjoy.

If you have no need for a motorized wheel, don't go to

the expense, even for a bargain. It is, after all, another electric appliance demanding energy. Certainly don't spend for two-speed school model type electric wheels. There's not enough speed gradation for smooth throwing and they are really costly for what they are. My choice, if the wheel is a necessity, is to use the $200 for a used reliable name electric wheel.

Taking care of your wheel initially is a kindness, and comes back to you with benefits over the long haul. This is especially true with motorized wheels. They're easier to maintain than the most basic car and can last fifteen years or more even with constant production use. Clean up the head after heavy usage. This will avoid clay encrustations around the shaft. Make sure that the wheel is always level. Leveling the wheel when you place it initially will prevent wobbles, distorted pieces, early aging, and heavy wear and tear on the wheel. I use a carpenter's level to check it out now and then. Place it across the wheel head and check in several directions. Compensate for floor unevennesses by shimming. Check out your belts or rubber parts every few months. Dustcovers are not really necessary though some people use them as a matter of course. My underlying assumption in this chapter has been that you are using your wheel every day.

VII

Glaze

A glaze is a glass that has been adjusted to stick onto a pot.

Chemically, a glaze is composed of a silica oxide plus a melting agent, added to promote fusion below the normal melt point of the silica, and some alumina oxide to stiffen the mixture to the point where it can hang on to a clay body. Alumina is usually added into the glaze mix in the form of clay. The glazes you will apply to your pots are usually mixed up of dried chemicals (in a powdered form), and an appropriate amount of water. While these raw materials are suspended in the water, the glaze is applied to the pot by dipping, pouring, painting, spraying, or a mix of methods. The porous, bisqued pot soaks up the water. The powdered glaze chemicals hang on to the surface of the vessel.

The creation and handling of glazes is not as mysterious and insurmountable as beginners sometimes believe. If you can get your head into thinking of a glaze in terms of three basic items—silica for glassiness, a flux or melting agent, and some clay for its alumina contribution—you can begin to understand the primary families of glazes and how to go about creating your own.

Once you've grasped the concept of the three chemical needs of a glaze, you must ask yourself what temperature you intend to fire your planned glazes to. Kiln temperature determines much of glaze behavior. If your only available kiln is a small electric kiln, for example, with nickel-chrome alloy elements, your glazing temperature shouldn't exceed 2000°F. You have to create low-fire glazes. Pick a temperature, such as cone 04, and plan around it. If you have an electric kiln with Kanthal elements, you can fire at higher temperatures. It is extremely important to settle on a specific temperature range. You will teach yourself a lot more in a short time by limiting yourself to a particular firing temperature. Firing to a different temperature every time you set out to glaze fire will have you in the trial and error stages for a disproportionate amount of time. The temperature decision you make will determine which kinds of glazes you will produce. Certain chemicals don't function well at certain temperatures. Some fluxes such as lead are particularly useful at lower temperatures, but are fugitive and problematic at higher temperatures. There are fluxes active only at high temperatures and thus useless for low-temperature work.

Another determinant in glaze behavior besides chemical composition and temperature is kiln atmosphere. In a natural-fuel fired kiln the potter has three kinds of fires available to him: an oxidizing, clear flame, a reducing or smoky (carbon) flame, and a neutral fire that is somewhere between the two extremes. An oxidizing flame is characterized by complete combustion, due to a fully adequate supply of oxygen. Coloring oxides in the clay and glazes do not yield oxygen to the combustion process because there is in the atmosphere enough available for burning. As a result, the clays and glazes relate roughly to the simple color of the metallic oxides in them. For example, iron glazes are tan to rust brown when they come out of an oxidizing fire, roughly like the red iron oxides used to color them.

A reducing fire is one that is starved for oxygen. This is achieved either by the potter cutting back on the air supply deliberately or by an overabundant fuel feed (sometimes even an almost uncontrolled increase). The oxygen decrease forces the excess carbon in the kiln atmosphere to hunt for an oxygen supply. The carbon finds its needed oxygen in the metallic oxides present in the clays and glazes of the wares. It then snatches up whatever oxygen it can get from them and in this way *reduces* the metallic oxides to their base metals. The metallic coloring oxides yield their oxygen to the combustion process. As a result of this interaction the glazes usually take on colors characteristic of the metals themselves, not their oxides. Using iron as an example again, you will see glazes that are cool gray, gray-green, bluish-green, olive, etc., resulting from red iron oxide colored glazes that have been fired in a reducing atmosphere.

When electric power is used, no reduction proper takes place. Numerous people have experimented with creating a smoky atmosphere in an electric kiln. They do it by introducing into the kiln near the height of the firing process such carbonaceous matter as pine slivers, sawdusts, or mothballs. If you wish to do this kind of reduction, prepare yourself by selecting for your kiln the best ventilated position in your workshop and expecting a very short element lifespan. For someone potting on a very tight budget this is an experiment beyond your financial reaches. You'll blow your kiln elements too frequently for your money resources.

Local reduction can be achieved in electric firing by the introduction of carbon into your glaze mixture itself. This is usually done by the addition of silicon carbide to the base glaze. You cannot, however, expect the generalized achievement of reduced clay bodies and glazes throughout your kiln when attempting to create a reduction atmosphere by these methods in your electric kiln.

What really goes on in an electric "firing" is a heating process that does not rely on burning for the release of heat energy for heat build-up. Without ongoing burning you cannot create a sustained carbon-hungry atmosphere. Heat increase proceeds in an electric kiln, in the presence of an adequate oxygen supply, i.e., the air in your kiln. No excess carbon attacks wares for those oxygen molecules in the coloring oxides. Since the metallic oxides are not solicited for their oxygen content, they remain comparatively stable (not reduced to base metals), and yield colors characteristic of the oxide form. In other words, clays and glazes fired with electricity will look like clays and glazes fired in an oxidizing natural-fuel fire. Or, theoretically, they will look alike.* In an electric firing the heat rise is not generated by burning. There is no constant fire to promote a more chemically reactive atmosphere. The entire complex range of oxidation-reduction interaction is eliminated. So when it comes to glaze results, atmospheric factors are nowhere as important in electric firing as they are in fuel firings.

From this point on, I am assuming that you understand the atmospheric differences and their degree of relevance or irrelevance to your own firing conditions. The question

---

* Theoretically, they should look alike, but in practice they often turn out looking quite different. My recent experience with LPG firing (with crude homemade burners) leads me to believe that the clear bright oxidizing atmosphere I see is a relative thing, not totally clear and oxidizing. For the same glazes that I have been using for years in electric firing situations turn out decidedly different, softer and somewhat reduced looking. I think that my crude burners, with very primitive air control, tend to make for a slight reducing fire at all times, even though the more obvious signs of reduction, smokiness, etc., are absent. This would account for substantial differences. I think a slight reduction is very common in studio firing situations, even when not specifically sought after. Of course, I'm pretty glad about the changes. But keep this all in mind if for some reason you're trying to get glazes that need an oxidizing atmosphere out of a natural-fuel situation. If you're trying for some oxidation glazes in a natural-fuel firing, use saggers.

of atmosphere and firing is complex and properly belongs to a book that deals with fuel-fired kilns. This chapter will deal mainly with the primary factor: the chemical makeup of your glazes. I will go into glaze chemistry from a purely experiential point of view. Part of my material will deal with the problem of glaze names and classifications. Many people are just put off by the endless fog of terms, names, and categories of glazes.

Studio potters have benefited greatly from the standardization of materials, language, computation principles, and technique that industry has developed, but on the whole work very experientially when it comes down to the nitty-gritty. For purposes of intelligent chemical substitutions, efficient buying, extension of the color palette, and total grasp of the intellectual underpinnings of their craft, most studio potters have assimilated the principles and methodology of the unity formula and the "empirical" method of glaze calculation. Excellent discussions and explanations of this approach are to be found in Glenn C. Nelson's *Ceramics* and Daniel Rhodes' *Clay and Glazes*. I feel these are essential tools for the independent, self-sufficient studio potter. I also feel this material is simply above the heads of novices, recreationally or therapeutically oriented potters, and anyone lacking three or four years of solid potting activity.

I think it is much more crucial for a beginner to get into those bottles of magic powders. Get to know the raw material intimately and experientially; what it does wet, dry, and fired, and how it feels in all those states too. It is best to collect glaze recipes rather than read formulae. A glaze recipe is a statement by weight of the ingredients in a particular glaze. A formula is a statement in terms of molecular proportions of the ingredients. Collect recipes appropriate to your kiln's temperature range. Test constantly, every time you do a glaze firing. I suggest making all glaze adjustments on the basis of *your own experiential* findings, as opposed to abstract calculation. You can do this within a framework of reasonable limits if you teach yourself the major characteristics of your basic raw glaze materials. At the back of this chapter there's a listing of the more important (frequently used) glaze chemicals. Familiarize yourself with the list, their common natural sources, their activity range, unusual properties. I have some process suggestions for rational testing that I want to get on to.

Clear the categories from your head and prepare to get into the labor and delight of glaze testing. Don't do anything without a notebook or stack of 3″ x 5″'s handy. Glaze testing and compounding take many man hours. Don't waste your time by testing and not keeping records of the results. Glazing will involve all kinds of beneficial accidents, surprises, and inexplicable events. Keeping records cuts down the need to duplicate tests when you've had a happy accident, provides theoretic grounds for explaining results, and gives information about your kiln's behavior patterns. You don't need to master the abstract system of glaze analysis to keep track of what you are doing.

It's really important to establish a fruitful dynamic between controlled experimentation and random creation. The most beautiful and fecund glazing in ceramic history and man's spiritual life has come from an integrated dynamic of discipline, experiment, and chance; not from the modern industrial approach to glazing.

TESTING

The first physical thing to do is to roll out many, many slab tiles. When they have completely dried to the touch, bisque fire them. Number the tiles systematically with something that won't burn out: an underglaze pencil or slip of a color that contrasts to the clay body color. On the *unmarked* side paint a creamy mixture of water and one glaze material—one solitary chemical. Do a tile for every compound listed at the end of this glaze chapter and for every frit or other material you have purchased or have been given. List the tiles numerically in your record book and write down what material you've painted on the correspondingly numbered tile. Fire these tests to your projected glaze temperature. Very few of the tiles will come out of the glaze kiln looking glazed. Most will have a thin layer of fired material just sitting atop the tile, with no fusion between body and surface material achieved at all. Some tiles will appear fluxed. These fluxed-looking tests will be various, depending upon the glaze temperature you have fired to. In this way, you will see what white lead, or colemanite, or a soda feldspar, do on their own, in a tangible firing. You may make discoveries. For example, you may find that the ball clay you bought (as a plasticity addition for your clay body) has the potential of a good white slip, all by itself. It may be a siliceous ball clay that can function as a slip up at the cone 4 to cone 9 firing range, with no other additions. After your raw materials testings, it may appear firmly fused to the clay body but dry, unglossy, and not glazed.

Testing a bit of every raw glaze compound may seem tedious to you, but it will tell you a lot more about the substances you will be using every day than all the listings of "most commonly used ceramic oxides" put together. All the instructive and descriptive lists abound in the better books but they seem to mean little to beginning potters—just more words. So order, unpack, separate, test, handle, and sieve all these oxides, with and without water. Then they will become your familiars. There is little point in teaching yourself glaze calculation or computation if you have no concrete feeling for these "commonly used" materials.

Now get out your triple beam balance, the gram scale; it can measure from one tenth of a gram of stuff to two and a half thousand. Balance the scale at zero. Add your scoop and counterweight if you have them. Otherwise, place a light plastic bowl on the scale plate and make a counterweight for that container of any handy material: wire, cardboard, wood, etc. Balance the scale at zero again. Measure out 100 grams of something by moving the marker on the hundred beam to one hundred. Then, spooning your raw material into the bowl, add material until the pointer returns to zero. You've weighed out your 100 grams of x. Pour the stuff back into its jar. Set the marker at another amount—20 grams, for example—and weigh out the new amount of the second material. When the pointer returns to zero again, empty out the contents of the weighing bowl back into the original jar. Move on to a different substance. Weigh out 100 grams of your third material, and then a fourth, fifth, etc., noticing that 100 grams of different materials look very different in volume, the amount of space taken up in your measuring bowl. Do this measuring routine until you feel completely at home with the scale. There isn't anything complex involved with the use of gram scales. It's simply a more precise and exacting measuring device than most people have had occasion to use.

Later on in the book, I discuss how to order supplies. I always suggest quantity ordering for someone who is setting up a studio, whether individually or with a few other people. Large quantities are very much cheaper than small amounts and allow the potter to test freely. Make test batches of 200 grams of recipes that seem right for your chosen temperature. This is twice or even four times the amount normally recommended for tests but I justify it with the fact that 50-gram test batches give suggestive but unfleshed-out results. Small tests don't reveal much. If the test looks potentially good, you wind up mixing all over again, in double the first quantity, for still another test firing. A new base may look fine on a small tile, but turn out too runny or problematic or disappointing when applied to a sizable vessel. It sounds wasteful of materials recommending such large test batches for the first go round, but in the end it saves labor, frustration, and material. After a while you develop a sense about new base recipes. On the basis of your own experience with your own kiln you will carry rough proportions in your head in regard to new glazes. You will be able to eliminate certain new recipes that come your way without concrete testing, just on the basis of too little alumina or some such characteristic that strikes you as off, in the written recipe. Below is a base to be tested and fired to anywhere between cone 4 and cone 8.

Weigh out the required amounts of the ingredients in your chosen recipe. Usually, recipes list raw materials by actual weight. It is a proportional statement in concrete, measurable terms. For example:

Spodumene (a lithium-bearing spar)	20	grams
Dolomite	20	
Flint	20	
Ball Clay	20	
Frit (3124, 3134, whatever you have as long as it's leadless)	20	
total	100	grams

To mix a 200-gram test batch of this recipe, you must double the amount of each ingredient: weighing out 40 grams of each material. This is a recipe for a raw batch of a base glaze. The base contains no coloring agents (no metallic pigmenting oxides), no opacifiers, no textural additions; only the stuff to make it glassy and fused and able to cling chemically to a pot.

MIXING

When you have weighed out the 200 grams, place the five ingredients in a large bowl, add water slowly to the dry ingredients. Less than an 8-ounce cup of water will probably yield a good, creamy mixture. Pass the wet mix through an 80- or 60-mesh sieve. After sieving once, sieve again, and a third time if the consistency has not evened out totally. This is simpleminded, boring but necessary work. *Wet sieving disperses all the glaze ingredients evenly throughout the mixture and homogenizes the consistency.* It is impossible to get good, informative results from a test batch that is too lumpy or inconsistent to go on a pot evenly. If you don't sieve your glazes well it is impossible to get good glazing results from your quantity mixes after the testing stages are over.

There are alternatives to sieving. You can do it once and get to like unevennesses, surprises, erratic good and bad results from the same glazes. You can grind the ingredients with a mortar and pestle. I find this really tedious and unproductive with amounts over 100 grams. You can grind the ingredients in a ball mill. A ball mill is a mixing device that consists of a porcelain jar loaded with flint pebbles. The jar is mounted, motorized, and rotates when the motor is started. The turning action rotates the flint pebbles which grind the glaze evenly and thoroughly. Ball mills are not cheap. They are not too useful for testing because you often do not know how much water (exactly how much) is needed for your new glaze. You can tell roughly, but all raw glaze materials absorb water at different rates. The best way to deal with the unknown absorbency factor of a new mixture is to add water a little at a time and be very conservative. When the consistency is such that glaze coats a dipped finger evenly, like cream, and drips off very slowly, it's probably about right. Not too scientific, and an awfully general rule open to a thousand modifications, but you'll get to know the feeling through constant finger immersions. This procedure is not recommended for raw-lead based glazes.

Back to ball mills. They are costly and can grind only one glaze at a time. In the same few hours you can sieve many. Unless you come into ball mills free, sieving is what you come back to.

Some glazes work well only in thickly applied consistency. Others may be better thinly applied. You find this out to some degree by testing your new batch of a base through applying the glaze both thickly and thinly on the same test piece. Dip your test pot or tile or shard into your newly sieved, creamy 200 grams of glaze and water. When the glaze has dried, dip a portion of the same piece again. That's it, right over the first application. Upon drying, the twice-dipped part (it has a very thick application of glaze) may show pinholes or cracks forming in the glaze coating. Note this in your test records. For test purposes, leave these marks *alone*. When you unload the tests from the glaze firing, check out the twice-dipped portion of the piece. If the cracks or pinholes are in no way visible in the fired piece, have fused out completely, you will know that your new glaze has a wide tolerance for thickness of application. If, however, your glaze has pulled away in a pattern of globules leaving the old cracks exposed as unglazed patches on the finished piece, your new glaze has "crawled" as a result of overly thick application. You can store this up in your mind, or notes, and perhaps use it as an intentional textural variation for a future piece. You should not use such a thick application of a glaze of this sort on utilitarian ware.

Food will get stuck in the unglazed veins and be hard to get at in cleaning, an unsanitary nuisance. Crawling is commonly regarded as a major glaze defect and should be avoided on all utilitarian pieces. The same holds true for pinholing due to overly thick application. Defects sometimes turn out to be texturally useful on the right pieces, but you are doing people a disservice if you give them supposedly functional pots that turn out to be arty nuisances.

Testing of this sort tells you much more about a new glaze than painting on a bit of test tile. Try to test recipes on a real pot whenever possible. If your throwing is not proficient yet, you can pinch-pot dozens of little shallow vessels very quickly, just for tests. Bisque and number these (with an oxide or a contrasting slip). Whenever you glaze a numbered test pot with a new base or color variation, write down the number of the pot, the recipe used (noting any substitutions or variations you make on the original recipe), and the date of the test firing. Keep a file or notebook of these tests. After a while you won't be able to keep all your results in your head. So start with some plain method of recording your results, before you find that you're forgetting or confusing test results.

Once you have fired some sample pieces glazed with the new recipe to your chosen kiln temperature, you confront your results. If the base is well fused, even, hard, smooth to the touch, relatively resistant to scratching or abrasion, shows no network of cracks (a sign of tension between glaze and clay body) and no other defects, and has achieved what you aimed for in surface quality, i.e., mat or glossy, a good working tolerance of applications (from thick to thin), you have the basis for many glazes. If your new base doesn't answer to these requirements, adjust it or test another base. Do not start testing color variations or textural variants *unless the base functions*

well in all the essential points listed above. It is a waste
of time to try to work out colors or other problems in a
base that doesn't work well from the start. I'll return to
adjusting a promising base that doesn't quite make it.
For the present, let's assume your tested base turned out
well.

If your base is transparent to start, you may opacify
it and create a white glaze by adding tin oxide, a zirconium oxide-based opacifier such as zircopax, or titanium
dioxide. Titanium will opacify to some degree, but it will
also change the base in a refractory direction (make it
more mat), or add a yellowish color to the base. It may
make the glaze more mat or even dry and underfired-
appearing if added in large quantities. Tin and zircopax
opacify without changing the base radically. Tin oxide is
very expensive but it is used in comparatively small
amounts; 2 to 5 percent added to a base will opacify it
substantially. Tin, however, will influence certain color
reactions in a glaze. Zircopax must be added in large
percentages, 7 to 10 percent. Titanium may be added in
the form of *rutile*, a combination, impure ore made up of
iron and titanium. Five to 10 percent of rutile will usually
opacify a transparent base and produce a white that is
definitely cream-colored or opalescent. Using rutile is a
way of adding titanium without having to worry about
changing the essential quality of the base. The iron seems
to offset the refractory tendencies of the titanium. My
preferences in compounding white glazes that have to
be fired in electric kilns run to combinations of tin and
titanium dioxide. Five percent of each (10 percent altogether) produces eggshell-colored whites that are smooth,
opaque, and rich.

Still assuming that your base functions well, your next
interest will probably be in creating colors. There are
many different metallic oxides to add as pigmenting agents

for colored glazes. For color tests you can weigh out a 1000-gram batch of your base. Do not add water; this happens dry. Put the 1000-gram batch of your base glaze into a gallon jar. Close the jar tightly and shake up thoroughly the raw glaze material. Put the jar down and let the powders settle. Open it up and then sieve the ingredients through a 60-mesh sieve, dry. Shaking up the stuff and then dry sieving it will disperse the ingredients evenly. Now, weigh out ten 100-gram batches of the base glaze. Put each 100-gram batch into a small jar (baby food jars are perfect sized containers for this), or a sandwich-sized plastic bag. Put a label onto each jar, or in the bag— "100 grams base X plus ____% of ____." You will weigh out and add different coloring oxides to these miniature batches and eventually fill in the blank labels:

> 100 grams of Base X plus 5% of *red iron oxide*—#1 (of series).
> 100 grams of base X plus ½% of *cobalt oxide*—#2, etc.

Start adding the colorants to the small batches by weighing out the metallic oxide that theoretically yields the color or colors you're after. Roughly:

> For electric kilns:
> tans, rusts, browns, ambers, blacks—iron oxides
> blues—cobalt oxide, cobalt carbonate
> greens—copper oxides, copper carbonate, chrome oxide
> purples and mauves—manganese carbonate, manganese dioxide, cobalt saturations
> yellows—vanadium stain compounds (tin plus vanadium oxide, usually), uranium oxides (if you can get some and are firing low)
> oranges—rutiles, red iron oxide, crocus martis (a crude iron oxide), uranium again
> blacks—combinations of copper, cobalt, manganese, or iron oxides.

I said roughly, because the chemical makeup of your base influences the color behavior of these pigmenting oxides. The specific colors you achieve will be the result of a combination of your kiln's behavior, the influences of your chosen bases, and your personal preferences.

The oxides are added in small percentages over and above the ingredients in the base recipe. For example, ½ percent of cobalt oxide (which is very strong) will color almost any base blue. If your test batch is 100 grams, compute the cobalt addition as follows: ½% of cobalt oxide = .005. One hundred grams of the base × .005 = .5 grams of cobalt to be added. Only five-tenths of one gram of cobalt oxide are needed to color your 100 grams of base blue. A stronger color would come of using 1 percent of cobalt oxide: 100 grams of base × .01 = 1.00 or a gram of cobalt oxide. One percent of cobalt oxide will usually yield a strong, sometimes strident blue. In most bases, 1 percent of cobalt is too great an addition. An overly large dose of cobalt may produce a black, metallic-looking glaze. If you like the result of your 1 percent cobalt test, you may feel like mixing a greater quantity. If you were mixing 500 grams of glaze, you would compute the color addition for the strong blue as follows: 500 grams of base × .01 = 5.00 grams of cobalt to be added to the 500-gram batch of the base.

Few coloring oxides are as strong or as stable as cobalt oxide. Most of the metallic oxides that are used as colorants are added in greater quantities than ½ percent or 1 percent. If you wish to produce a warm, brown glaze, you would turn to red iron oxide for pigmenting. Try an addition of red iron oxide for your first 100-gram test: 100 grams of base × .05 = 5.00 grams (red iron addition). Add 5 grams of red iron oxide to the 100 grams of the base. Wet sieve the test several times to distribute the color evenly and then apply the colored mix to a small test pot. Color testing of a previously tested base may be done on test tiles or small pots because you already know many major things about the glaze's fundamental behavior. At the end of this chapter there is material on coloring oxides, descriptions, percentage recommendation. Every oxide will react differently with a different base. So all such material is general and just meant as rough reference stuff. One of the crucial points to keep in mind as you color test is that most of the coloring oxides you use also tend to act as fluxes when added to bases. In small percentages they do not essentially change the base glaze. In large amounts they can radically alter the melting behavior of a glaze. Large amounts of several oxides added to one base, together, will often produce a metallic black. Overly large additions promote extreme runniness and a very metallic or highly glossy surface in most glazes. The only exceptions to this are in cases where the base glaze itself has been created with the specific purpose of its being able to accept a saturation of colorant additions. Part of the glaze's flux is calculated as stemming from the colorant oxide(s).

A good working base glaze can yield glazes of differing surface quality as well as glazes of differing colors. Changing a semi-gloss base into a mat glaze is possible, as is changing a mat into a gloss. Such changes are not usually accomplished by a simple addition of an oxide to a basic recipe. Changing the mat or gloss quality of a glaze involves altering the refractory to flux ratios of a glaze. In most instances, a glaze can be made glossier, shinier, or smoother melting by increasing the flux and decreasing the refractory content, the alumina content in particular. Translate that into the materials you use: decrease the clay content in your base recipe and increase the fluxing oxides. Conversely, a mat finish is encouraged by diminishing the flux oxides or increasing the clay (alumina contribution).

The way to experiment with these sorts of changes in an already established base is—timidly. Decrease the fluxes by a small amount, 5 percent or less. Add clay in small amounts, barium too. Record carefully any tests of this kind. If you alter the base glaze in any significant way, from extreme gloss (for example) to semi-mat, let's say, expect your color responses to change from those of the original base. I call this kind of adjustment juggling. It is not the recommended technical procedure you will find advised in most ceramic texts. It works well though if you have firsthand experience of these ordinary ceramic chemicals. You can make adjustments of this kind on the basis of a few facts: what does this raw material contribute to a glaze? Flux, silica, alumina, or combinations of the three and how much? The quantity question can only be answered by the reference material you have on hand, analyses from suppliers, or textbook data.

Textured glazes may be created by drastically changing the base recipe in the direction of immaturity. In other words, add a great deal of a fusion-resistant (refractory) material, such as kaolin (china clay) or barium carbonate; and the glaze will come out of the test kiln looking unfused, underfired, very dry, often rough, cratered. Within limits (too immature and the glaze ingredients will fall right off the surface of the piece), many sculptural textures can be created. These cratered, blistered, dry glazes are a total disaster on pots that are supposed to be functional wares—mugs, teapots, etc. Cleaning pottery with surfaces like that is next to impossible and pretty tough on the dishwasher's hands.

Once you have compounded, tested, fired and used a small palette of reliable glazes stemming from your *one* functional base recipe, start on a new recipe. Two or three workable bases can yield hundreds of glazes.

Often electric firing tends to give only reliable, reproducible, similarly surfaced and similarly textured glazes. If this is evolving as a pattern in your work, try:

glazing over freely painted slip decoration

painting with oxides and slips over freshly glazed pots

pouring one glaze over another (two relatively thin coats)

varying your methods of glaze application

adding granular oxides to your existent glazes—such as granular manganese dioxide or granular rutile or ilmenite

refiring once-glazed ware at still lower temperatures after redecorating with overglaze enamels or lusters

experimenting with colemanite as a replacement for some of the fluxes in your current glazes

extending your color testing and testing with more combinations of colorant oxides

doubling and tripling some of the recommended limits for colorant additions

using wax resist.

Wax resist is a decorating technique that relies upon wax's ability to block out water or mixtures suspended in water. After glazing a bisque pot, paint a freehand design with liquid paraffin or a wax emulsion. After the wax dries, hold the pot by its foot and pour a second glaze over the entire piece. The second glaze will run off the waxed areas. When the piece has dried, fire it. Your first glaze will appear (from under the now burnt-out wax) as a contrasting pattern in relation to the parts of your pot glazed with your second glaze. Wax resist painting may be done directly on the bisqued pot. Glaze the pot. After the firing, the waxed areas will appear as unglazed, clay body areas, and will contrast both in texture and color with the glazed parts of the piece. The decorative potential of this technique is great. Try not to glaze too heavily if you're planning to use two different coats of glaze.

In the matter of greatly increasing the colorant additions: take care but try it. Test any such experiment (10 percent or more oxide addition) on a control tile. This will save any kiln accident from becoming a disaster to your kiln in general. Glazes that utilize a saturation of colorant oxides are not uncommon. They are costly. Coloring oxides are relatively your most expensive pottery need after fuel or power considerations. Glazes that make use of 5 percent of cobalt oxide or 15 percent of red iron oxide will make your budgetary instincts wince. If, however, you are interested more in color than in brown pots, save your bread up to buy oxides in quantity and then experiment with saturated bases.

APPLICATION

It is hard to believe the importance of physical application to successful glazing. Many glaze defects and dissatisfactions arise from poor or inexperienced glaze application. Some glazes don't work or fuse properly as a result of poor application.

Don't paint glazes onto pots. Painting is the technique that will assure you of the most uneven application. Unless you have a very specific, textural concept in mind, don't brush on glazes. In painting, the brush deposits a substantial amount of glaze at first and less and less toward the end of the stroke. It seems economical in some ways but will always produce a thick and thin covering of glaze. If you wish to use this as a pattern—paint. Do paint with

slips or mixes of coloring oxides and water. These will
bleed through your overall glaze coating and chemically
interact with the glaze. Many individual and beautiful
pieces evolve out of this kind of decoration.
The basic methods used by studio potters for applying
glazes are: pouring and dipping. Pouring glazes onto pots
is economical (it doesn't require very large amounts of
glaze on hand), and has good decorative potential. A variety of application through pouring thick and thin coats
onto a pot produces very individual and diverse surfaces.
Pouring takes practice. To achieve a basic and even coating of glaze on your bisqued ware will take much repeti-
tion. Practice by filling a few straight-sided glass jars with
water. Take some other variously shaped glass jars and
think of them as "pots." Pour the imaginary glaze (water)
onto your practice "pots" by pouring around the pieces.
Move your hand around the practice piece as evenly as
you can. When you think that you have achieved an even
rotating motion, start glazing some real pots by pouring
around them. Don't expect to get a perfectly even coating
on your first pots but keep on aiming for more and more
evenness. After your pots are evenly poured, you can start
experimenting with thick and thin pourings and then double pourings of different glazes. Be careful not to pour
overly thick coats when doing double pouring.
Dipping requires larger amounts of glaze on hand than
does pouring. Dipping produces very even results and
these can be varied too: redippings, pouring over dipped
first coats, poured designs that are dipped over, and painting over dipped pots. Dipping is done by holding the
bisqued pot by the foot and rapidly plunging the pot into
a bowl or bucketful of well-mixed glaze. The inside and
outside of pieces can be glazed in one rapid swoop, known
as double-dipping. After immersing the pot, give it a quick

turn (it's still under the glaze), and the glaze will rush up into the inside of the pot, coating it evenly and quickly. Pull out the piece and you will find the inside and outside smoothly coated with glaze. This should be done fairly rapidly. For large amounts of ware and matched pots (plates, bowls, mugs, etc.), dipping provides the simplest, most reliable, and quickest glazing results for the individual studio potter.

If you plan to produce really great quantities of matched wares, you should look into building a spray booth. Personally, I think spraying shouldn't be dumped on as much as it is among studio potters. Industry has had a monopoly on the use of spray application and most individual potters have thus been down on spraying for a long time. Their basic claim has been that spraying has resulted in the most constantly boring, mass-produced sameness in pots. In the last few years, however, many studio potters have utilized spraying for sculptural pieces that have anything but a "mass-produced" quality. There are a number of very creative potters who are making use of this technique in nonindustrial, new ways.

For people planning on making a living from matched wares or certain large-scaled items such as fountains or big lamp bases, spraying may turn out to be much more convenient than dipping or pouring. In terms of economy of materials, you do lose glaze material in spraying. You must also have a well-ventilated spray booth (and the room for it in your workshop). It is possible to build a serviceable spray booth very cheaply. Do consider the costs of a compressor and spray outfit, which are substantial. Unless you have a very well thought out production need or sculptural requirements, I suggest staying away from spraying as a basic method of glaze application. But do take a look at the current use of sprayed glazes in the work of people like James Crumrine and Hui Ka Kwong.

The ideas you may have about industrial sameness are in for a jolt.

Often in schools, students are introduced to spraying as the first and basic method of glaze application. This is a kind of ass-backwards learning experience. Dipping, pouring, and painting teach you much more about the consistency requirements for a good glaze coating than does spraying. When you are familiar with consistencies and coating thicknesses you can move into spraying and get good results on the basis of your past experiences.

Since I've brought up the matter of glaze consistencies, I wish to point out a few things about achieving an appropriate glaze consistency. The foremost factor in applying an even, suitably thick coating of glaze to a bisqued pot is the *physical condition* of the glaze. In the section above on "mixing" I've described wet sieving for mixing test-sized quantities of glaze. Every glaze you mix in quantity for general use should also be *wet sieved two or three times* before it is applied to a single pot. Dispersing all the glaze chemicals evenly in the mix and homogenizing the consistency of the glaze by sieving will assure you of a reliable, even coat when you pour or dip the pots in the stuff. If your glazes have been standing around for any length of time, *stir them up* and *resieve* them thoroughly in preparation for your glazing session. Stirring alone is not enough. Resieve all the glazes that have stood around, even those that have been unused for only a couple of days. You will see how settled, lumpy, and uneven the mixtures become from non-use. Reconditioning glazes is a time-consuming activity, but an absolute must for good glaze results.

The second major part of glazing properly is the amount of repeated experience you bring to the pouring, dipping, and decorating. When you have achieved glazing competence, you can start more freewheeling experimentation.

SOME MORE BASIC SUGGESTIONS

Elaborate on only a few bases. This will teach you more about your fundamental chemicals than hopping from recipe to recipe. Adjust on the basis of experiences with your own kiln. Watch and record closely anything you do with these few bases. For the purposes of experience, extend any good, working base in every direction you can think of, make it glossy, make it mat, make it opaque, make at least ten different colors. You may not even like some of the variations that result, but do it for the experience. You will know an awful lot about handling that particular glaze when you're through.

Try to use related families of glazes. I've found that this evolves naturally. If you fire above cone 4 or 5, you tend not to use lead. You would probably use spars as your basic fluxes. If this is your case, purchase one soda spar when you order, and one potash spar. Substitute the ones you bought for others specified in your collected glaze recipes. This will help familiarize you with the behavior of the two spars and will help keep your glazes chemically related, should you get into overpourings of different bases or paintings of one glaze atop another. Or, if you're using frits, keep it down to one or two. Substitute yours for what recipes call for. If you fire low, purchase one lead frit and one non-lead frit. That's really all you need. Keeping the purchases down is economical and teaches you more.

By following these recommendations you will get to the primary factor in glazing, an experimental understanding of the materials you work with and depend upon. First try to get to this awareness for the basic raw materials and then for the coloring oxides. Money, time, and your kiln are your limitations. Work with them creatively. Understanding the implications of these limiting factors and matching that understanding with an intimate knowledge of the chemicals and how they act will make it possible for you to interact with the complicated dynamics of glazing instead of being overwhelmed by them. After a year or two of this kind of practical experience, teach yourself the abstract, chemical approach. There is a workbook available that deals exclusively with *Glaze Calculation*, that is the best thing I've seen for someone who has some knowledge about the processes and materials, and who is teaching himself. The final mysteries will not be solved by your learning the chemistry of what you've been doing, but it is essential for intelligent ordering, buying, substitution, general comprehension, and creating from scratch from your favorite natural substances.

A DIGRESSION INTO THE CLASSIFICATIONS FOG

You have to be able to consult books and periodicals and friends with some background. Classification, names, terms seem to present a problem for many people when it comes to gathering glaze information. So that we all know what we're talking about in common, I'm making a categories digression.

As described above, glazes are glasses that have been changed with a view toward making them stick onto a clay body or ceramic vessel. These specialized glasses are influenced by *chemical makeup, temperature determinants,* and *atmospheric conditions.* Since there are so many factors involved in glaze-making, glaze descriptions, classifications, and names have multiplied in all directions. When a person new to clay technology tries to get into glazing, he runs head-on into a wall of terms. To simplify the matter, try arranging these names in relation to one of the three major glaze determinants I have listed above.

Some glazes are named for reasons of *chemical composition*. Usually an important, active material, such as the flux, is singled out and gives its name to a grouping of glazes. Such a group would include the *feldspathic* glazes, largely dependent on feldspar for flux; or *frit* glazes, those utilizing frits as major fluxes; or *colemanitic* glazes, heavily dependent on naturally occurring calcium borate (colemanite) for a flux. These have been named for convenience purposes after an active chemical agent in the base. People are always talking of "lead" glazes, "alkaline" glazes, "lead-free" glazes, "lead-borosilicate" glazes. Don't be put off by these labels. They only refer to some chemical contributor that dominates the character or behavior of the glaze. It's convenience jargon.

The second classification grouping is based on *temperature*. The temperature that is important for classifying purposes is the maturation point temperature: the point at which your clay body and glazes reach their most complete body-glaze unity, final color and density, and other ultimate traits. Glazes are constantly referred to as "high-fire" or "low-fire" glazes or "medium-range" glazes. This too is self-explanatory. A low-fire glaze is one that matures at a temperature that is commonly accepted by potters as "low." That is all there is to it. What constitutes high or low among potters is an open subject. Confusion sets in where names are used in an overlapping way. When a glaze is called "low-fire," at some point and then two minutes on in your text the author is calling it an "alkaline" glaze, it seems weird. Actually, the glaze-maker has simply told you more about the glaze. It is an alkaline-dominated glaze that matures at a low temperature.

The third grouping is the most tangled. Glazes that are named for *atmospheric* factors don't usually explain themselves. A "celadon" glaze doesn't describe its origin in its name. It belongs to the atmospherically influenced grouping because it can only be produced in the presence of a reducing fire, in a reduction atmosphere. Celadons are also "high-temperature" and "feldspathic" glazes, but the quality that really sets them apart is that they are dominated by the various reactions of iron oxide obtained in a reducing atmosphere. Other specialized glazes that are dominated by atmospheric conditions are high-temperature "copper reds," reduced metallic lusters, and salt glazes.

Salt glazes are extremely individual. Here the atmosphere counts for almost 90 percent of the glaze's behavior. Salt glazes are formed by introducing common table salt, sodium chloride (NaCl), in quantity, directly into the kiln chamber at the height of the firing. The salt must be thrown in when the clay body is nearing its maturation temperature. The sodium can then combine with the active silica in the clay to form a thin, textured, glassy coating on the surface of the wares. The gases in the kiln include vaporizing hydrochloric acid, so stay reasonably clear of the ports and flues. As you can see, such a glaze is almost totally conditioned by the atmosphere.

All useful rules have their exceptions. Aside from the three classifying groups I have arranged, there stand *raku* glazes. Raku is a ceramic process evolved originally by Japanese potters and widely used to produce wares for the tea ceremony. Raku is greatly influenced by Zen principles and aesthetics. It is a process dominated by an extraordinary direct, rapid, glazing technique. Bisqued raku pieces are placed into a preheated, red-hot kiln, their glazes allowed to fuse, and then pulled from the kiln immediately—the potter using long tongs and asbestos gloves. The red-hot, glazed pieces may then be subjected to various kinds of reducing procedures. In any handling, raku is dominated by the rapidity and shock qualities of the action. Specialized clays or clay bodies are used: compounded to withstand the shock of sudden heating and cooling without cracking apart. Raku glazes are low-temperature glazes created for this unusually demanding process, frequently using lead as the prime flux.

CAPSULES OF EVERYONE'S FAVORITE OXIDES

A. Silica

—the glass-former; chemically we're interested in silicon dioxide, SiO_2; the primary raw materials that yield silica for pottery purposes are: flint, feldspars, clay.

B. Alumina

—alumina controls the fluidity factor in glazes, stiffens them up; the theoretic oxide is Al_2O_3 and its primary source is clay, all kinds.

C. Flux Oxides

1. Feldspars: nonsoluble, naturally occurring, cheap abundant providers of potassium (K), sodium (Na), calcium (Ca), *oxides*, the major active fluxes, plus other goodies thrown in are Al_2O_3 and SiO_2:

potash spars: $K_2O \cdot Al_2O_3 \cdot 6SiO_2$
soda spars: $Na_2O \cdot Al_2O_3 \cdot 6SiO_2$
lime spars: $CaO \cdot Al_2O_3 \cdot 6SiO_2$
(theoretic)

Lithia minerals provide lithium oxide for flux, unusual
color response, problems with high thermal expansion:
   Spodumene: $Li_2O \cdot Al_2O_3 \cdot 4SiO_2$
   Petalite: $Li_2O \cdot Al_2O_3 \cdot 8SiO_2$
   Lepidolite: $LiF \cdot KF \cdot Al_2O_3 \cdot 3SiO_2$

2. Other naturally occurring compounds providing flux
oxides:
   Colemanite—$2CaO \cdot 3B_2O_3 \cdot 5H_2O$: the most convenient provider of boron oxide in near-insoluble form and
CaO at the same time, a high-activity flux with a wide
range of action; colemanite glaze behavior could be a
book in itself.

   Dolomite: a double carbonate of calcia and magnesia,
yields two important active fluxes, and it's cheap and has
a wide temperature activity range too.

3. Compounds yielding one major fluxing oxide:
   a. Barium carbonate; convenient source for barium
oxide, a strong flux up at high temperatures, refractory
down low, important for the creation of mat glazes.

b. Talc: a cheap naturally occurring source for magnesia oxide plus silica.

c. Zinc oxide: very active flux up high, increases firing range and gloss, very good for some bright color responses and some opacification capacity.

d. Whiting: this is calcium carbonate, a major source of CaO, a really important high-temperature flux.

e. Lithium carbonate: a source of lithium oxide, very valuable flux in the middle-temperature ranges and at high temperatures, beautiful responses with copper oxides.

4. Lead oxides: the world's most widely used low-temperature fluxes; produce glossy, well-melted glazes, always come through, reliable and cheap, found as the following raw materials:

litharge (lead monoxide, PbO)
white lead (lead carbonate, $2PbCO_3 \cdot Pb(OH)_2$)
red lead (Pb_3O_4)

Highly poisonous if ingested continually (even in small amounts, cumulative in the human body), or if constantly leached out of finished wares by food acids and eaten regularly. Use it in a fritted form if you can.

5. Boron oxide: B_2O_3, actually a neutral R_2O_3, but seems to act like a base (fluxing metal), wide-range flux, available in highly soluble raw materials like borax as well as in the comparatively insoluble form of colemanite, and, of course, in fritted (nonsoluble) form. For an amplified discussion of the complex role of B_2O_3, the reader should see Michael Cardew, *Pioneer Pottery*, p. 57.

D. Frits: man-made compounds that provide useful oxides in a form that does away with toxicity and solubility problems. See the wordlist for definition and further explanation.

These are the fundamental materials and oxide sources you will need to make your own glaze bases. When you order for the first time, use this list as a purchasing guide. Order the cheapest forms of the materials. Use this as a reference outline to study the descriptions of the important oxides in other texts, such as Rhodes or Nelson. Use the spaces provided under each capsule to write in notes on your own fired samples of the material as described in the beginning of the glaze chapter.

E. Coloring Oxides
1. Iron family colorants: a very big family, all oxides of iron (Fe); they're common, cheap, easily mined and refined:
    Red iron oxide
    Black iron oxide
    Rutile
    Ilmenite
    Crocus martis
    Iron bearing clays: Ochre, Barnard, Albany slip clay.
In an oxidizing atmosphere the iron family yields browns, ambers, oranges, russets, yellows, tans, creams, beiges, mottled surfaces and opalescences (rutiles), a huge diversity of warm earthy tones.
In a reducing atmosphere iron produces cool colors: olives, blue-greens, grays, gray-greens, celadons, subtle gray-whites, again a huge palette of variations. Start your experiments with 2–3% in reduction, more if using an iron-rich clay (5%).
In oxidation, 3–10% for oxide additions and 10%+ when adding iron-bearing clays.

2. Cobalt family: strongest, most stable responses of all the coloring oxides, use small amounts, starting as low as ½ to 1%, available in the forms:
Cobalt oxide and cobalt carbonate.

3. Copper group: Greens, turquoises, all related combinations of blue-greens are produced by copper additions when fired in an oxidizing atmosphere. Reds are achieved by reducing copper-colored bases at high temperatures. Anywhere from 3 to 5% of copper oxide or copper carbonate is effective. I use red copper oxide in smaller amounts (2%). The available forms are usually:
Black copper oxide and copper carbonate, sometimes red copper oxide.

4. Manganese oxides: 4 to 7% of manganese dioxide or manganese carbonate produce violets, winey purples, tans, browns, blacks (mixed with another oxide).

5. Nickel, chrome, vanadium oxides: less intensively used than the ones listed above. Consult Rhodes. Reliable yellows are usually obtained by employing commercially prepared tin-vanadium stains.

F. Opacifying Oxides

1. Tin oxide: expensive but the most effective opacifying agent, beautiful color responses, changes the character of the base very little, 3–5% additions.

2. Titanium dioxide: opacifies but in the direction of cream whites or yellowish whites, refractory tendency in large amounts, 3–5% additions.

3. Zirconium oxides: not as effective as tin but much cheaper, good, hard, tough surfaces, 8–10% additions at least for definite opacity (still cheaper than tin).

4. Zinc oxide: may be used for some opacifying but not in quantity; it will substantially alter the behavior of your base.

G. Infrequently Used Oxides

1. Uranium compounds: good for producing yellow, orange, or red glazes at low temperatures (lead bases best), very costly and usually hard to get.

2. Cadmium and selenium oxides: not as hard to get as uranium oxides and used for generally the same colors and same temperature range; this too is a costly venture.

3. Oxides of rare metals, gold, for example: not hard to get in the prepared luster preparation but very expensive.

It is not necessary to order everything the first time around. Your economic and space limits will be good guides, in addition to your chosen kiln temperature, collected glaze recipes, proximity to sources, and general past potting experience. You can produce a great variety of colors from the following theoretic order:

1 lb. red iron oxide
1 lb. cobalt oxide
1 lb. black copper oxide
1 lb. copper carbonate
1 lb. manganese dioxide
2 lbs. rutile
2 lbs. tin oxide or 5 lbs. of zircopax (or other zirconium-based opacifier)
1 lb. vanadium stain (or substitute 1 lb. chrome oxide or 1 lb. nickel oxide, depending on your own color predilections)

Starters: a glaze recipe collection

I—cone 4–cone 7 colemanitic bases

HIGH GLOSS BASE
Flint	30
Kaolin	5
Feldspar	20
Talc	14
Colemanite	32

GLOSS BASE
Feldspar	45
Kaolin	30
Dolomite	30
Zinc oxide	30
Colemanite	15

MAT BASE
Potash spar	45
Flint	30
Kaolin	15
Dolomite	15
Colemanite	30

SEMI-MAT BASE
Potash spar	60
Flint	15
Kaolin	15
Barium carbonate	30
Zinc oxide	15
Colemanite	15

II—cone 4–cone 7 lithia bases

SEMI-GLOSS BASE
Spodumene	20
Flint	20
Clay	20
Dolomite	20
Non-lead frit	20

SEMI-MAT BASE
Spar	47
Flint	40
Dolomite	18
Kaolin	3
Zinc oxide	18
Lithium carbonate	4

MAT BASE
Petalite	20
Flint	20
Dolomite	20
Frit (non-lead)	25
Clay	15

MAT BASE
Soda feldspar	57
Kaolin	8
Barium carbonate	18
Flint	2
Whiting	11
Lithium carbonate	4

III—cone 4–cone 7 Albany slip clay bases (deeply colored bases)

MAT BASE
Albany slip clay   70
Nepheline syenite 40
Barium carbonate   10

THIS BASE YIELDS A DEEP BROWN GLAZE.
Variants:
    tan—10% rutile addition
    black—2% cobalt oxide
    Olive brown—2% copper oxide and 5% rutile

GLOSS BASE
Albany   90
Colemanite   10

(PLUM) GLOSS BASE
Albany   70
Yellow ochre   10
Frit (non-lead) 20

IV—cone 04 bases

Non-lead frit 80
Kaolin   10
Zircopax   10

Lead frit 3304 100
Ball clay   10
Zircopax   20

Colemanite   80
Yellow ochre 20

Non-lead frit 20
Kaolin   5
Cryolite   70
Flint   5

—all these bases tend toward glossiness

V—cone 9–cone 10 bases

Feldspar 33
Flint   43

IRON SATURATE BASE
Buckingham spar   54
Flint   22.5

Kaolin   10
Whiting 14

Feldspar   44
Whiting   20
Cornwall stone 20
Kaolin   6
Calcined kaolin 6
Zinc oxide   4

IRON SATURATE BASE

Kaolin   6
Whiting   13
Barium carbonate 2.5
Zinc oxide   2.5
    add 5% red iron oxide
Soda spar   42
Colemanite 12
Dolomite   6
Talc   15
Kaolin   5
Flint   20
    opacify base by
    adding 3% tin oxide

—the bases of group V will vary in surface quality according to the specific feldspars chosen and eventual glaze firing conditions.

VI—cone 9–cone 10 Albany slip bases

Albany clay will fire to a pleasant brown glaze at this temperature with no further additions. If you're interested in some variants:

ALBANY BLACK
Albany   90
Nepheline syenite   5
Cobalt oxide   2

ALBANY GOLD
Albany   90
Nepheline syenite 5
Titanium dioxide   5

ALBANY OLIVE
Albany   90
Whiting   10
Black copper oxide 3

ALBANY MOTTLED AND
    SPECKLED
Albany   100
Red iron oxide   5
Rutile   5

VIII

Buying and Selling and Cycles

It seems to be better to pay more attention in the beginning to buying than to selling. You can eventually sell more pots to more people cheaper if you do the selling directly and the buying economically. You are freer to experiment and explore materials unknown to you if you buy in a planned quantitative fashion. Always buy in quantity; raw materials by the ton at least, two and a half tons at a time if you can get that together with some people. Quantities of material on hand make you less precious when testing, more daring when creating new clay bodies or glazes, and more deeply acquainted with the mysterious powdery substances. Buying clay dry, in ton quantity, allows you to pass the reduced costs on to people who buy pottery from you. When you order clays for your clay body, add to the order at least 50 pounds of each of the following: one ball clay, one kaolin, flint, whiting, Albany slip clay, Barnard clay, barium carbonate, colemanite, dolomite, and a feldspar (two if you have another $3 to spare, one soda and one potash). You can add a few extras if you have another $10: a talc, nepheline syenite. These are the basic raw materials you will need for glazing. You can bring in a dry material ton for $100 or $120 (depends on your clay selection). This sounds like a lot, but compare it to the $200 you might spend for

133

prepared clay, not to mention what your oxides will cost you over and above that. Most studio potters expend $100 or more easily in one year's supply buying, and get less for their dollars.

Try ordering cooperatively with other potters. When doing this, make sure to work out details regarding the transportation of delivered materials in advance of the actual freight drops. Work out ordering details carefully and try to order under one letterhead, in typed form, as completely as possible in one shot. Plan for the materials division in advance too. If it always falls to one person to do the orders, transport, and materials division, it's not very cooperative. Large firms accustomed to industrial wholesaling will not bother with trifling $5 orders, illegibly presented. Buy wholesale and make sure to buy with a local retail sales tax number so that you don't pay retail taxes on materials you use for making objects that you, in turn, retail.

There are suppliers listed at the end of the book. If you are in a hard-to-supply locale, contact local universities, industrial ceramics and refractories concerns in your region, the American Crafts Council, for regional info. Request technical data when planning to do quantity ordering. Even if it doesn't mean anything to you now, file it. It will mean something soon.

Be on the look-out for secondhand buys on chemicals, particularly coloring oxides. Many would-be potters outfit themselves splendidly with entire glaze chemistry laboratories and then discover it's all too dense for them. I've bought a whole studio's glaze setup for under $10. Be up on your raw materials' current pricing to know whether you're getting burned or not. Don't buy or take anything that looks totally unfamiliar (color, texture), that is unlabeled (might have been mixed-up for all you know), or from a completely unheard-of source. Secondhand chemicals are most cool when still in the vestiges of their original packaging.

Keep records of purchases and sales, and label things. If you're into minimal verbalization, keep all buying and selling records in the same notebook with your glaze notes and researches. Staple into the same book any bills, price lists, useful information. Such a ledger is guaranteed to blow the mind of your local IRS agent.

At this point in time there are few alternatives to supporting a small going pottery in any other way than selling the pots you make. Few communities are economically well-based enough or have evolved to a labor diversification point where they can support a pottery and potter(s) simply for the spiritual luxury of a steady supply of unique, handmade pots. Some communities, such as alternative schools, can incorporate a functioning pottery as a skills exchange center. All in all, though, most potters still keep the bus on the road by teaching (for money) other people to pot, or by selling many, many small-scaled utilitarian objects.

My feeling about this kind of selling and teaching is that it's best to keep both (or either) to an absolute minimum, doing only enough to keep you, your community, and your pot shop going. Putting a ceiling on the production pottery trip becomes necessary so as to have time to explore new forms, create new colors, grow.

Try to sell directly to people rather than through the traditional retail outlet. Outlets mark up 100 percent over your usually rock-bottom, wholesale price to them. They have put handcrafted pieces out of the money-reach of most people and have put heavy production demands and timetables on supposedly individual craftsmen. It is time for a craftsman-dominated marketplace that is not presided over by the spirits of American merchandizing presumption. Boycott outlets. Make your own—by selling straight to your buyers, or in common with other crafts-men direct to people, or by trading. We only need enough to pot on.

If you sell right from your workshop, be alert to local retail sales tax regulations. Sales tax bureaus can hassle you legally; to be kept in the back of the head when ad-vertising or selling. Check out prices in pottery shops and retail stores in your area. You can sell at half their prices and still make enough to eat and go on potting. Most craftsmen get only about 50 percent (maybe two-thirds if really big names) of what looks like a really high price in a fancy store; some get less.

Try fairs, if transportation is feasible. Seasonal sales right on the workshop premises are good for potters. The selling can be arranged to coincide with the end of a heavy glazing cycle. People dig seeing where and how things are made. After the sale, you're free to get back to some more potting. Street selling from a cart or van has potential, if legal in your area. Find out about the licensing routines, or you may find yourself ticketed. Time out here for cheers for NM, our nine-year-old VW transporter. It's done more than its share of hauling and truckin', up to 1700 pounds at a time (we don't recommend that as a steady). We don't drive over 45 mph. and don't do over 1200-pound loads anymore. Street selling usually moves small, inex-pensive pots. Transporting large pieces around the streets for long periods in stop-and-start situations will involve some breakage.

See if you can provide a wide range of pots for persons interested in buying; a wide range from small to large, good to excellent, utilitarian, decorative, and sculptural. You turn more people on if you offer a diversity of kinds, forms, colors. Don't take complicated orders until you're really proficient and they're easy to turn out. Take orders on the basis of specific glaze samples in your workshop and on the basis of pots on hand; not on the basis of nebulous forms and colors that may turn out to have been envisioned differently by potter and buyer.

You can concentrate on making better pots and sell them much cheaper than those of big stores if you don't have big overhead anxieties. Keep your basic workshop overhead low. A cheap rental, or no rental at all, is the prime factor in overhead struggles. Firing costs can be handled by selling your "seconds." Selling seconds provides pottery to people who dig handmade pots but who haven't the bread to buy "firsts." Be consistent in your seconds thing. Label them as seconds, explain why they are if you get the chance, and include all pieces with glaze defects, surface cracks, all pieces that are firing "accidents" no matter how curious or useful. These tiny sales really add up and help toward the utilities bills. The sale of seconds also develops a wider audience for pottery because buyers learn a lot when purchasing seconds. It's weird, but people do ask more questions about a thing obviously gone wrong than about the firsts they buy. After a time you will produce fewer and fewer unintentional seconds. I kept the bin full by discarding glazes and combinations and tests that I had decided against. There are always a few pieces out of every kiln that just don't make it, not for technical reasons so much as for aesthetic considerations.

Still, saving money by doing little things is important. Cart your own trash out, recycling what you can. Wash your own plate windows and make your own tools: cutters, calipers, modeling sticks, mops, bats, wheel heads, wheels. You can evaporate most of the factors retail stores add up to produce their huge overhead figures.

CYCLES

Potters' work goes in cycles. Rhythm, relation, and satisfaction seem to make for better pots and happy potters. Clay must pass through distinct phases of existence in its passage from slime to transcendent form. These separate states determine much of the potter's work rhythm and consequently part of one's life rhythm. It's crucial to work with large groupings of pots or families of pots, tribes of sculptures. Certain pots will evolve more perfectly than their brothers. The potter can see his work in a constantly growing context through the evolution of these families and the development of their better and lesser representatives. Differences, similarities, changes, and maturations involve the potter and constantly renew and enlarge the potter's relations with the primary stuff, clay.

The working rhythm is dominated at first by the act of shaping and forming. Most people think of this as the "creative" part of ceramics. I feel it's one among many creative acts in ceramics; so are firing, glazing, preparing clay. But since your workshop is, in time, given over at first to the formation act, it seems preeminent. Actually, drying, firing, living, all must be in your consciousness while handling and forming the plastic clay. It's a matter of tuning your awareness to the whole process.

Drying is a slow releasing of the water physically combined with the clay. It comes directly after the activity of the ware formation time. It offers a meditative opportunity in which to consider the more completed forms, watch their physical changes, think about the behavior of the chosen clay, and arrange one's head about the preparation and execution of the first firing.

The bisque firing places the potter in relation to the kiln. It is in some ways a time of submission. If your work has been technically careful and your stacking and firing attentive, the pots emerge from the bisque structurally intact and transformed. Rest your head after the unloading and then get into your pots' new phase. They look ghostly because of the pale, immature biscuit color, compacted, changed yet incomplete.

The glazing of these new but unfinished-looking pieces must be preceded by a time of thoughtful consideration of each pot's potential and then by an equal period of active, even frenetic preparation of glazes. Leave lots of time for weighing, sieving, mixing, and applying glaze. Don't try to rush through the mixing work or you'll make weird errors in weighing and compounding. It is precise, even minute, work; so plan lots of time for it. The application of glazes and decoration of pots can evolve as an eased time of concentrated intense action if all the setup work is allowed for. Play and gravity can both surface in proportions that express where you are at, in this time and place. It is a kind of painting in theoretic dimensions. The water-glaze suspensions, used when applying glaze, don't look anything like the later, glaze-fired, finished pottery surfaces. You have to envision physical and chemical magic being worked on your pot in the fire and relate to the inner processes. You can do this with some degree of control and you can also work to encourage happy, random transformations that are unique and unreproducible.

Let your glazed wares dry. While this happens you can prepare your kiln furniture and kiln chamber for a glaze firing. Wash the shelves with kiln wash. Clean out bits of clay or any other debris from the previous firing. After the shelves are thoroughly dry, arrange your pots and kiln supports for stacking. Attend your firing. Try to get into the changes taking place in your kiln and in your works: molecular shifts and recreations, atmospheric metamorphoses, changes from liquids to gases, entries, exits, and passages. Even if you are firing an electric kiln, try to stay with it and out of other shop work. You watch time and heat climb more closely. You get to know your kiln and clay and glazes well. Kiln color becomes meaningful to you and you build up the experience needed to gauge firing by color. When you become intimate with fire you understand its transforming power. If you give yourself up to it in this way, it releases its secrets and transforms with you, instead of acting like an uncontrollable variable. Cracking a glaze kiln marks the end of a cycle. A period of reflection sets in while you wait for enough heat to escape slowly for you to unload. Fruition and a return to forming again both appear during the unloading. The surprises and finished works always engender new ideas, suggest variations, reveal what were dead ends, and start of themselves the entire rhythm again.

Today, it's basically a personal cycle. Past cycles in pottery had great seasonal relation and relations to nature, agriculture, and human change . . . pottery past was predicated on integrated communal involvement. This last is what we don't have yet but what a lot of people are trying to move toward. What I've done with my life was to reintegrate it around my work rhythm. It's not hard to do in ceramics and not narrowing because you're always working with all the fundamental elements: earth, fire, air, water (even in citified, overly thinned-out forms). Work is becoming something other than what we were all guilt-conditioned to do with our time. Perhaps it's becoming part of the new life cycle.

BOOKLIST

The ceramic bibliography has zoomed in the last six or seven years, a fact that really delights me. I thought you'd like to know about the books I found most informative during those dry times I was teaching myself the basics. The starred books represent my choices for the studio reference shelf, real tools.

Bjørn, Arne. *Exploring Fire and Clay.* New York: Van Nostrand Reinhold, 1970.

For clayworkers interested in, or needing access to, very primitive firing technology—kiln designs, materials, firing practices—this is an essential tool. For other potters—those into higher firing ranges, etc.—it's a kind of birthday goodie. The book is written from an archaeological perspective but contains explicit information and many useful illustrations on the subject of building and firing primitive wood-burning kilns. If hole-in-the-ground wood-burning kilns are not your trip, get the book from a library one day.

* Cardew, Michael. *Pioneer Pottery.* New York: St. Martin's Press, 1970.

In my opinion, this is the most complete and beautifully comprehensible book in the English language on potting, to date. It retails around $16; a very, very stiff price. For persons who are in isolated situations and who want or need one fine, all-around book that emphasizes digging and processing your own clay and glaze materials and sophisticated wood-firing technique, this is it. It is an absolutely lucid, unembroidered, no-shit book. If you have no prior potting experience and are not yet into country potting, digging your own clay, etc., don't rush out to buy this as your first book.

You may find the text not pertinent and even leaving you behind in many instances. It will all mean something one day; treat yourself to it then.

Colbeck, John. *Pottery: The Technique of Throwing.* New York: Watson-Guptill, 1971.
This is a good throwing manual, comprised of serial photographs and a minimum of text. There is good material and emphasis on clay preparation. The photos are poorly keyed to the text but the content and illustrations are the best I've seen. It is priced at a steep $10; but if you have no teacher to help you with your throwing this will fill some gaps.

* Goldberg, Steven A. *Glaze Calculation.* San Jose, Cal.: Billiken Press, 1970.
This deals *only* with the material suggested by the title. If you've had a few years' potting experience and can understand the formulaic methodology outlined by Rhodes or Cardew, get hold of this and use it as a companion piece-laboratory manual for teaching yourself glaze chemistry. It's a good substitute for programmed classes in glaze chemistry, but is definitely not for pottery novices.

International Lead Zinc Research Organization. *Lead Glazes for Dinnerware.* New York: ILZRO, 1971.
A manual that deals with the knotty problems of achieving resistance of lead-glazed utilitarian pottery to food acids. If you plan to make any low-fired dinnerware that employs lead glazes, better write the ILZRO at 292 Madison Avenue, New York, N.Y. 10017, and ask for a copy.

* Leach, Bernard. *A Potter's Book.* New York: Transatlantic Arts, 1948.
Leach's book is a fundamental informational tool for the studio potter. It is also a revolutionary document. Let this be your first potting book and you'll always find yourself coming back to it. There's a lot of potting experience and technique packed into its pages, as well as a clearly articulated belief in the evolution of the spirit through the vehicle of handcrafts.

* Nelson, Glenn C. *Ceramics: A Potter's Handbook.* New York: Holt, Rinehart and Winston, 1966.

The second edition is an expanded and improved work and one of the best general reference books to have on the studio shelf. It has all the reference tables, data, and informational material you might need. Most of my students have found it much more readable than Daniel Rhodes' *Clay and Glazes,* though I think it is not as comprehensive and fleshed-out as the Rhodes book. I personally am put off by the quantities of photos and the layout, but many people I know have found the profusion of photographs a true asset. If you can locate the paperbound copy you've got a good reference tool.

Norton, F. H. *Ceramics for the Artist Potter.* Cambridge, Mass.: Addison-Wesley, 1956.

This is a good, if a little old-fashioned sounding, comprehensive, well-written and well-structured handbook. Should it come your way secondhand, add it to the shelf.

Reitz, Don. "Salt Glazing Technique" in *Salt Glaze Ceramics.* New York: American Craftsmen's Council, 1972.

For people wanting to know about, or get into, the salt revival.

° Rhodes, Daniel. *Clay and Glazes for the Potter.* Philadelphia: Chilton, 1957.

My preferences put this at the top of the list of studio reference material. It is the most developed and comprehensive of the American-oriented technical books. Stylistically, it is nowhere near the literate and lucid quality of the writing of Leach and Cardew, and that puts a lot of beginners off. But Rhodes has everything in there you need to know to get functioning, cached in there somewhere, even if his style doesn't make for easy reading.

―――. *Stoneware and Porcelain.* Philadelphia: Chilton, 1959.

This is both a technical book and a philosophical statement expressing the author's feelings about the aesthetic preeminence of high-fired ceramics; clearly worth looking at even if you're not doing cone 9–10 reduction fired stoneware, but not an absolute reference shelf necessity.

―――. *Kilns: Design, Construction and Operation.* Philadelphia and New York: Chilton, 1968.

Most people (see the LWEC review), feel this to be the definitive kiln-building book. Before making a heavy monetary or emotional investment in this book, check out Paul Soldner's ACC pamphlet, *Kiln Construction*. If you're planning to fire with LP-Gas, use this book as an ancillary tool, not your Bible. On the plus side, there's simply no other text in English that brings together so much kiln-building experience or detailed information.

Richards, M. C. *Centering: in Pottery, Poetry and the Person.* Wesleyan University Press, 1964.
Not a technical book; just what the title implies.

Riegger, Hal. *Raku.* New York: Van Nostrand, 1970.
A beautiful book; costly but pertinent for anyone seriously interested in pursuing the technique and tradition of raku.

Sellers, Thomas. *Throwing on the Potter's Wheel.* Columbus, Ohio: Professional Publications, 1960.
A paperback cheapie and helpful, though not as evolved as the Colbeck throwing guide. Available from Stewart Clay Co., 133 Mulberry Street, New York, N.Y. 10013.

* Soldner, Paul. *Kiln Construction.* New York: American Craftsmen's Council, 1965.
I've found this to be the most useful work available on kiln-building. It has little historical material and no pretensions to ultimate detail, levels with you all the way about how many details you'll have to fill in yourself; it's got all the basics and then some. It also marks the introduction to the ceramic literature of the living and breathing, artist-built catenary arch kiln. It is short, to the point, well-organized, and organically structured.

Wildenhain, Marguerite. *Pottery: Form and Expression.* New York: American Craftsmen's Council, 1959.
Primarily, a beautifully illustrated philosophical and personal statement.

Periodicals to check out:

Ceramics Monthly, 4175 N. High St., Columbus, Ohio.
—often very hobbyist oriented but lots of useful clay body and glaze recipes and miscellaneous information.

Craft Horizons, American Craftsmen's Council, 29 West 53rd St., N.Y.

—expensive but profusely illustrated magazine that ranges over all the contemporary crafts scene.

Pottery Quarterly, Northfields Studio, Northfields Tring, Herts. England.

—a well-produced, unpretentious small journal that contains informative, studio-potter oriented articles and good photographic illustrations.

—and I hear tell of an American *Studio Potter* magazine coming in on the winds soon.

SUPPLIERS

No listing contained in a book, published at a certain time in a specific place, can be definitive or fill everyone's needs; I make no claims in those directions. I do know, however, that finding supply sources is a big hassle when you're first setting up on your own. A fairly comprehensive list, which is periodically brought up to date, can be secured from the American Craftsmen's Council at 29 West 53rd St., New York, N.Y. 10019. Ask for the list entitled *Suppliers: Clay.* My own list is much less inclusive, tends not to include many hobby-oriented supply houses, and bears witness to my quirks, preferences, gaps, geographic limits, and experiences. Starred entries represent firms whose products or services I've used and been really pleased with.

A. D. Alpine Co., 353 Coral Circle, El Segundo, Cal. 90245.
  —well-established suppliers of equipment: kilns, wheels, etc.
° Babcock and Wilcox, 161 East 42nd St., New York, N.Y. 10017.
  —refractories are their business: bricks, kiln furniture, cements, "Kaowool" (an alumina-silica insulating blanket).
° Carborundum Co., Refractories Division, Box 337, Niagara Falls, N.Y. 14302.
  —the source for silicon carbide refractories: shelves, etc., and also the manufacturer of "Fibrefrax" products; a line of alumina-silica insulating blankets, cements, felts, etc., that represent a new technological breakthrough in kiln insulation. (See also Babcock and Wilcox, above.)
° Ceramic Color and Chemical Mfg. Co., New Brighton, Pa. 15066.
  —my long-time favorite supplier of colorant oxides, raw glaze materials, and frits. A quantity-only house, they were, in the past, extremely informative, reliable, rapid, and inexpensive.

147

148   POTWORKS

Unfortunately, as of this writing, they've gone over to a policy of not selling to studio-scale craftsmen, only to industrial businesses. A great loss for potters in tight times!

Clay Art Center, 40 Beech Street, Portchester, N.Y. 10573.
—good East Coast source for the Shimpo wheel.

Crusader Kilns, 1064 Butterworth S.W., Grand Rapids, Mich. 49504.
—builders of electric kilns that are incorporating an alumina-silica blanket in their line. I haven't used this kiln but if you're in the Midwest and are planning to use electric power, check out this one.

Denver Fire Clay Co., 2401 E. 40th Ave., Box 5507, Denver, Colo. 80217.
—everything you need is carried by Denver; an old reliable in the trade, but a big geographic haul to the Northeast.

Duncan Ceramic Supply, 5649 E. Shields, Fresno, Cal. 93727.
—a recommended West Coast general supplier.

* George Fetzer Ceramic Supplies, 1205 Seventeenth Ave., Columbus, Ohio 43211.
—a general supplier with very good prices on raw materials.

* Hammill and Gillespie, 225 Broadway, New York, N.Y. 10007.
—best general East Coast supplier for clays, bulk raw glaze chemicals, and crude coloring oxides, i.e., Spanish red iron oxide. No equipment. Informed, always reliable service but quantity orders are their thing.

H. B. Klopfenstein, Rte. 2, Crestline, Ohio 44827.
—maker and source for the Klopfenstein kick wheel.

Kanthal Corporation, Wooster St., Bethel, Conn. 06801.
—they know all you need to know about high-temperature electric kiln elements.

Leslie Ceramic Supply, 1212 San Pablo, Berkeley, Cal. 94706.
—West Coast general supplier.

Mandl Ceramic Supply Co., RR #1, Box 269A, Pennington, N.J. 08534.
—clays.

* Metropolitan Refractories, Tidewater Terminal, So. Kearney, N.J. 07032.
—New York City area distributor of A. P. Green refractories: brick, kiln furniture, fireclay.

Newton Potters Supply Co., 96 Rumford Avenue, W. Newton, Mass. 02165.

—East Coast general supplier, average retail pricing.

* Orton Foundation, 1445 Summit Street, Columbus, Ohio 43201.
—manufacturers and wholesale suppliers of standardized pyrometric cones.

Overton, Clarence—Earthworks, 72 Holland Avenue, Staten Is., N.Y. 10303.
—custom-built, solid wood or welded pipeframe kick wheels from someone in the New York City area, who knows what he's doing.

Randall Wheel, Box 744, Alfred, N.Y. 14802.
—maker and supplier of a good free-standing pipeframe wheel, not cheap; the Randall wheel can be motorized too.

Resnick Scale Co., 40 Wooster St., New York, N.Y. 10013.
—a local dealer for the Ohaus scale company; they also service scales, should you have the rare need.

Rovin Ceramics, 6912 Schaefer Rd., Dearborn, Mich. 48126.
—Midwest general supplier with a well-chosen line of good things, carefully selected: Shimpo wheel, Crusader kilns, Walker pug mills, raw materials, etc.

* Skutt and Sons, 2618 S.E. Steele Street, Portland, Ore. 97202.
—makers of a beautifully designed and precisely executed line of electric kilns, geared to the hobby market, but of superior workmanship and durability than most. Their line is not cheap and shipping tariffs are sizable. They make a good power wheel too, also at a stiff price.

Soldner, Paul, Box 91, Aspen, Colo. 81611.
—seemingly expensive but actually very worthwhile line of welded pipeframe wheels.

Standard Ceramic Supply Co., Box 4435, Pittsburgh, Pa. 15205.
—good general supplier, retail prices.

Walker Jamar Co., 365 S. First Ave., E. Duluth, Minn. 55802.
—producers of pug mills; a costly equipment investment, however you cut it.

Western Ceramic Supply, 1601 Howard St., San Francisco, Cal. 94103.
—general supplier.

Westwood Ceramic Supply, 14400 Lomitas Avenue, City of Industry, Cal. 91744.
—general supplier.

* Jack D. Wolfe Co., 724 Meeker Avenue, Bklyn., N.Y. 11222.
—general supplier, average retail prices.

INDEX

Material that I feel is adequately covered in the Wordlist or Booklist has, in many cases, been omitted from the Index.

Washing, 18, 58
Water, 57–58
Wax emulsions, 19, 113
Wax resist, 113
Wedging, 30
Wheel, potter's
  kick, 75–92
  power, 75, 93–95

Wiring, 54, 56
Work space, 53–63

Zen principles, 121
Zinc oxide, 124, 128, 130–132
Zirconium, 108, 128, 131
Zoning, 1, 53–54, 56